Hear what others are saying about *SPECIAL STRENGTH FOR SPECIAL PARENTS*:

"I finished reading Special Strength for Special Parents and it was great. You did a wonderful job with relevant thoughts with the stories and scriptures. I cried through some. It will definitely minister to many people...many you may never know about."

"I love your book! I read it cover to cover the first two days I had it."

"Absolutely love the format! Each Daily Dose, Observation, Anecdote, Intake Notes, Diagnostic Questions, Prescription for Follow Up are just brilliant. They give the book purpose. Even though testimonials are important, the author makes it a personal exercise, experience and discipline for the reader. Kudos to you!"

"Your book is useful for any parent who has to nurture any child. I plan to keep visiting your website and staying current with your work."

"I shared your book with a co-worker who went to your site and was near tears to have found what she's been wanting. Until now, she said, she could find nothing with a spiritual side and the understanding of another parent. Thank you!"

"The stories are just what a young mother faced with a diagnosis and crazy feelings racing around in her head will want to pick up and read. Thanks so much."

"I feel I have found a mutual heart-friend, one who knows exactly what I'm saying and understands my every word."

Special Strength
For
Special Parents

31 Days of Spiritual Therapy for Parents of Children with Special Needs

NINA FULLER

---

www.GMApublishing.com

Published by GMA Publishing, Evansville, Indiana.

Our books are distributed worldwide. Order our books via
any bookstore or Amazon.com, Amazon.UK.com,
BarnesandNoble.com or most any other bookseller.

For more information about GMA Publishing products, or
publishing opportunities, visit our web site at
www.gmapublishing.com.

ISBN: 1-59268-075-5

Printed in the United States of America.

All Scripture taken from NIV unless otherwise noted.

Book Artwork Created and Donated by:
Brad A. Maglinger
BradMaglinger.com

Author's Photograph by Memories At Home
www.memoriesathomephotos.com

Dedication

To my beautiful daughter, Joannah Tess Fuller. Without you I never would have begun this special journey. You are a special gift from the Master Designer.

Acknowledgements

Life-long thanks go to Dr. Linda Ramsey and Robin Smith for saving both my life and my unborn baby's compromised life. We are "living proof" of your convictions on the value of every human life.

Thanks to Florence Littauer and Marita Littauer and CLASS Services for their expertise in so many areas.

Special thanks to Mike Fichter and Indiana Right to Life for giving me opportunities to share my personal experience throughout the state of Indiana initially.

Thanks to my representative at Ambassador Speaker Agency, Gloria Leyda and President, Wes Yoder, for believing in the power of my story and my abilities to be effective in touching hearts and changing lives.

Thank you, Anthony and Crystal Obey at GMA Publishing for the professional and personal encouragement you have generously given me on this project.

Thanks to special friends Jama and Waldo Parchment who opened their home to allow me time to clear my mind, seek the Lord and listen to His Word in order to convey it within these pages. Grand Cayman is inspirational!

Thank you to Brad Maglinger who is a talented, creative graphic artist who is at the top of his game.

Thank you to Rosemary Kniggendorf who accepted the challenge to use her editing skills to make this project concise, cohesive and credible.

Thanks a million times over to my husband, Andy, who not only has cheered me on but has put action to his words of support by becoming Mr. Mom to our children during this project in spite of his own very demanding ministry schedule.

Thank you to my older children, Jesse, Jake and Joey for their brotherly love and care of Tess and Hope and for the years of inspiration you have given me as your mother!

Special thanks to Mary Ellen Fuller, aka "Granny" for all the extra childcare and love you provided. Thanks, Mom!

Very **special** thanks to all the parents and siblings who share their stories within the pages of this book. They have made themselves vulnerable for the world to see their struggles and to share in their blessings.

Thank you to all of our ministry supporters who allow Andy and me to keep our hand to the plow. We covet your prayers and trust the Lord to bless your giving.

Thank you, Lord Jesus, for demonstrating Your love for me before I even knew you.
Thank you for seeing the potential in my life and making it useful for Your glory.

FOREWORD

As I scrubbed for the Cesarean Section and walked into the operating room in 1995, I knew I had a very sick mom and a very vulnerable baby with cardiac defects from Down syndrome and prematurity. What I didn't know is that both a ministry and this book were about to be birthed at the same time in this family...a family that I loved then and have only grown to love and respect more with each passing year.

It has been my privilege to be peripherally involved in several cases, like the Fuller family, who are vulnerable and kind enough to share their source of strength with the rest of us. If you love a great mystery and want to let God reveal the secret of life to you through the stories themselves, then read no further on this page and jump right into the first "Daily Dose" of *Special Strength for Special Parents*!

All babies, all kids, all people for that matter, carry messages. Sometimes, things go awry and lives are incomplete or unfulfilled in the destiny for which they were originally designed. You may be thinking I am talking about "special" kids...but I'm not. I'm talking about people who through choice and free-will choose to live apart from God and God's will. Kids are actually the real message-pure and unadulterated...straight from the heavenly mail chute. And special kids are the purest message we get. They're just written in another language...sort of like Morse code. All those dots and dashes don't make sense until you learn what the pattern means...and that takes time.

We who are followers of Jesus Christ live in two kingdoms. What looks like tragedy in this one, looks like divine planning in the other. What looks like suffering in this one, looks like purposeful activity in another. What looks like imperfection and disability in this one, looks absolutely stunning in their beauty and ability to accomplish the desires of God's heart in His Kingdom. And what seems incomprehensible in this kingdom...just a bunch of dots and dashes...is delivering the most valuable truths we are capable of knowing. Truths so profound that they can be carried in only the purest of vessels, uniquely fashioned for the Truth they carry from one kingdom to the other.

Linda Ramsey, MD, FACOG
Obstetrics/Gynecology
The Women's Hospital
Newburgh, Indiana

TABLE of CONTENTS

Introduction

This book is a gift to families! Sitting down with **Special Strength for Special Parents** is like sitting down with a friend who truly cares about you. Nina shares her heart and lessons of encouragement with her readers with empathic insight and spiritual wisdom.

The Scriptures used for the **Daily Doses** and **Observations** provide a foundation for daily living. Many are familiar, some obscure, passages that come to life when looking through the eyes of special needs.

Nina's personal **Anecdotes** about her family's journey are an encouragement to trust God through the doubts and victories of loving a special needs child. Nina shows realistic expectations of herself as a caregiver, as a mother, and as a wife, which is an inspiration.

The **Intake** and **Diagnostic Questions** Nina poses are suitable for anyone, not just those who have a child with special needs. Any reader will grow spiritually and personally by taking to heart the questions in **Special Strength for Special Parents.**

The **Prescription for Follow Up** is a resource that keeps the momentum going, allowing for personal application through your day.

The **Testimonials** from other families will allow the reader to realize that they do not have to be isolated in their parenting challenges. There is strength in shared experiences.

Special Strength for Special Parents is a thorough tool for family devotions, revealing thoughts and feelings that family members may have been hesitant to openly talk about until now, encouraging healthy personal and family relationships.

-    by Olivia King, LCSW, ACSW

Pre-Therapy Information

FULLER FAMILY TESTIMONY

Tiptoeing through our Super 8 Motel room, carefully avoiding the sleeping bags filled with three sons, a visiting niece and the family dog, I couldn't wait to get through the debris to the bathroom and take the EPT (early pregnancy test). I was anxious to find out if I was pregnant once again. We were en route back home after an enjoyable family vacation. I felt queasy all week as we camped in Gatlinburg, and I suspected I was pregnant.

Eager to be pregnant one more time, I took the "easy-to-read" test and was sure the blue line for "positive" would appear in the five minute process. 4-3-2-1. I made myself wait five minutes. No blue line. 6-7-8-9-10 minutes later there was the *faintest* line. "But," I thought to myself, "Maybe it's light blue for negative and dark blue for positive." Unsure of the analysis and disappointed at what appeared to be a lost dream, I sadly went back to bed since it was so early. "Lord, I just knew it would be positive by now. I don't understand."

What happened next became the theme for the following nine months – well, actually the last eleven years. "Trust Me. Trust Me. Trust Me." I heard. Not just one time ---three times for emphasis. I heard the voice of God speak to my heart and insist I trust Him with this desire to have one more baby.

An hour later, I again tip-toed back to the bathroom. I picked up the infamous stick and looked at it again. In the little window, as clear as day, there was no doubt. I was pregnant! I was giddy with joy! One more time, after three sons and a miscarriage, I was going to be a mommy again!

Little did we know at the time that God's emphatic whisper that morning would be the beginning of the journey I share with you throughout the following pages.

We have grown as a family, as husband and wife; our sons have grown into godly young men, and the two special daughters the Lord has given us have added immense joy to our family and our purpose in life. We are rejoicing in the Lord because we have trusted Him through each experience and we are glad in His salvation.

"Surely this is our God; we trusted in Him and He saved us. This is the Lord; we trusted in Him; let us rejoice and be glad in His salvation." Isaiah 25:9

I recommend you keep your Bible handy in order to read each passage thoroughly. Having an additional notebook handy will be good, too, in case you are inspired to put to paper the thoughts that have been simmering and are now at the surface.

I have included space for you to share some basic thoughts, but encourage you to continue beyond the space provided.

As you take time to read **Special Strength for Special Parents**, I pray that within these pages you will find spiritual strength for your continued journey in the world of special needs.

~ Nina

GIVE ME STRENGTH
ISAIAH 40: 1-31

"He gives strength to the weary and increases the power of the weak."

OBSERVATIONS

God is concerned about His people. He commands Isaiah to:
1. Comfort His people.
2. Speak tenderly.
3. Proclaim future glory of the Lord.

God, through Isaiah, reminds us of His character:
1. His power is seen through the fact His very breath can blow away man.
2. The word of God stands forever, in contrast to all else that will wither.
3. He comes with power.
4. He cares for His flock like a shepherd.
5. He gently leads those that have young.
6. No one compares even remotely to what God is capable of doing.

After a pivotal moment of personal accountability (verse 27), we are reminded of who God is:
1. He is the everlasting God.
2. He is the Creator of the ends of the earth.
3. He will not (now or ever in the future) grow tired or weary.

4. His understanding is beyond anyone.
5. He gives strength to the weary.
6. He increases the power of the weak.

Good news comes in the reminder that even youths and young men (full of energy and good health) will stumble and fall, and that all of those whose hope is in the Lord will:
1. Renew their strength.
2. Soar on wings like eagles.
3. Run and not grow weary.
4. Walk and not be faint.

ANECDOTE

Multiple times every day I plead with God, "Give me strength!" Sometimes, it's when my 10 year old with Down syndrome tells me, with an attitude typical of pre-adolescence minus the malice, "I don't think so," after I've asked her to get ready for bed after a wearisome day. Sometimes, it's when my 2 year old with Down syndrome has just unfolded all the clean laundry in the basket I just disciplined myself to fold. Sometimes, it's because the phone is ringing at 9:00 PM for the hundredth time that day, interrupting any hope of down-time I might have at the end of another demanding day.

The promise found in today's dose of Scripture is enough infusion of strength in itself. And yet, there is more, just like those ads on TV that promise "And if you buy today, you will also receive, absolutely free..." We are promised that we will "soar on wings of eagles." Wait! There is more, still! We will also run and not grow weary. Listen! For calling today, while supplies last (which we soon find out from Isaiah that the supply is everlasting) we will also receive the promise that we shall "walk and not faint."

I need these additional products of my hope in the Lord because I need to live like the eagles – above and beyond the chaos of those around me. I need to run and not grow weary from one doctor or therapist's appointment to the next, making sure I'm on time, even if the doctor is not, all the while aware that I have too much on my "to do list" than I can accomplish in myself. I also am renewed by the promise of being able to "walk and not faint" when my legs ache from the fibromyalgia which developed several years ago due to the incredible stress and compromised immune system I developed after my traumatic pregnancy.

I am reminded that my hope is in the Lord and not in my circumstances. This hope is not a false hope when it is placed in the Lord who does not grow tired or weary and has a reservoir of strength and power which He freely gives to those who hope in Him.

INTAKE NOTES

1. Circle or highlight any of these adjectives to which you can relate today: weary...weak...faint...tired...in need of comfort?

2. Have you been falsely accusing God of seeming not to care (verse 27)?

3. What are you are going through that might make you think God doesn't care about your cause?

DIAGNOSTIC QUESTIONS

1. Knowing that everyone, young and old, (verse 30) is capable of growing tired and weary of stumbling, what are the promises of those whose hope is in the Lord?

2. Which of these promises is most appealing to you TODAY? Why?

PRESCRIPTION FOR FOLLOW-UP

1. As a reminder, write here the six character qualities of God found in verses 28 to 29.

2. Take a minute and call upon the everlasting God who does not wear out but keeps going and going and going) who is ready to share His strength with you today!

Nina Fuller

A Bittersweet Journey
Hillary Key

There they were-- the words no parent wants to hear: "Your son has Joubert Syndrome. There are only 200 documented cases in the world. His brain stem is malformed. He most likely will not walk or talk-He will also have mental and sensory motor disabilities-that is if he lives beyond infancy."

This news came after two weeks of sitting in the NICU staring at the monitor that would alarm each time our sweet Bennett Daniel stopped breathing. His little body had endured test after test. With each result, the news seemed to get worse. Bennett had low muscle tone, vision problems, swallowing issues, reflux and a host of other possibilities. He also had unexplained episodes where his face would spasm on one side causing him to cry for hours from discomfort.

They had no answers. No answers we could cling to -- except this rare diagnosis. We were devastated. We excused ourselves to the hospital chapel. My husband, Jeff, looked at me and said, "That could have only been worse if he had said, 'and by the way, you're dying too.'" We prayed. I don't remember what exactly, but we prayed.

One week later, after three weeks of tearfully leaving the hospital without our son, Bennett came home -- along with monitors, oxygen, medication and an obnoxious list of specialists.

And so began the journey, a journey of bitter sweetness. The first months were more bitter than sweet. We mourned -- mourned "what should have been," mourned the struggles that were to come for our son. I wondered if there would ever be a purely sweet moment again. Would the joy of Bennett's hard-earned steps forward be tainted with the sorrow of knowing every milestone would come with great struggle, if at all? In a world pleased only with a perception of perfection, would anyone dare to be his friend? More importantly, would we even get to be with him long enough to walk him through these trials? The pain of our suffering child was too much to bear alone. These were questions only time would answer. These were answers we could only entrust to God.

God, in his grace, showed us He had not abandoned us. He poured out His love through the support of loved ones and through a Bible verse that reappeared in greeting cards and letters:

"Do not fear for I am with you. Do not be dismayed for I am your God. I will strengthen you and help you. I will uphold you with my righteous right hand." – Isaiah 41:10

We held tight to those words then as we do now. God has worked in my heart, giving me the ability to recognize more of the "sweetness."

Our son is a beautiful gift. He shows us daily miracles by facing obstacles with a smile, obstacles that would break most of us. His life is a gift that has taught me to take nothing for granted, to run to my heavenly Father immediately when I feel bitterness overtaking me, to treasure each moment, and mostly that the joy of loving and being loved is the best life has to offer. I've also learned sweetness overpowers bitterness.

Soon after we were given the news of Bennett's diagnosis, we were in the NICU sitting in front of Bennett's bassinet. Having no idea what Bennett's future would be, Jeff said, "I just want him to know I'm his Daddy, and I love him."

Bennett's first sentence was "I Luh Da Da" - one of many purely sweet moments. Every day before he leaves for work, Jeff hears, "I Luh Loo" and Bennett leaves for kindergarten. There, he is greeted by people who appreciate the gift he is. He is dropped off by a proud mom who smiles to herself knowing there is no limit to how bright her treasure may shine.

DAILY DOSE 2

PAYING IT FORWARD
PHILLIPIANS 1:6-11

"It is right for me to feel this way about all of you, since I have you in my heart; for whether I am in chains or defending and confirming the gospel, all of you share in God's grace with me."

OBSERVATIONS

Through a letter he has written to friends, Paul the Apostle shares words of encouragement with others, in spite of the fact that he is in the midst of his own crisis. Due to unfair circumstances (bogus indictment and consequent imprisonment), Paul has somehow found the secret of contentment no matter what his situation is. Let's take a peek into his letter:

1. He recalls the good times in spite of his current hardship.
2. He looks for something for which to be thankful.
3. He connects with God by praying.
4. He prays for others' needs even though he has overwhelming needs of his own.
5. He focuses on helping others (by writing the letter in the first place) instead of waiting for someone to do something to lessen his plight.
6. He speaks/writes positive words such as grace, peace, thanks, joy, instead of bringing others down to a level of gloom and depression.
7. He has faith (confidence as seen in verse 6) that God will finish what He has started in each person.

8. He humbles himself and lets others know that they all share in God's grace.
9. His words of affection are sincere before God.
10. He tells his friends what He has been praying for them (verses
11. He also tells them how these things can be achieved: through Jesus Christ.

ANECDOTE

Take a peek into another letter written in love and concern:

Dear Dad,

We received your beautiful card yesterday. You always find such special cards.

Dad, there is something I need to share with you about your unborn granddaughter. Andy and I and our entire family will be facing a challenge with this new life. We found out that we will be welcoming a special needs baby into our family. The test confirmed she will have Down syndrome. It has been an overwhelming shock to us but we are confident God has created this new life for a purpose and we will trust Him daily to give us strength and wisdom. We trust, too, that you and everyone else in the family will love our little girl just like any healthy baby entering the family.

There are many unanswered questions, Dad. Some will be answered in time; others, we may never understand. This is not what we had planned or hoped for but we know the Lord has great plans to bless everyone who comes in contact with our special baby girl.

*Jesse, Jake and Joey know their baby sister will be born with Down syndrome. They are remarkable in their acceptance and in their reaction to the news. Jake said, "God's Will is always best so this must be the **best**." Incredible wisdom and tenderness from an eleven year old boy!*

Dad, pray for us. We are committed to loving and raising each of our children the best we know how. For some reason, God has confidence in us to place a special baby in our home. I want to do my best to honor God and raise my children to be the best they can be, productive and well-adjusted adults in a crazy world. We will take one day at a time.

Our confidence lies in this, Dad: "And we know that in all things, God works for the good of those who love Him, who have been called according to His purpose" (Romans 8:28). We believe this with every fiber of who we are. I am so thankful to know God's love

Nina Fuller

everyday of my life. Just knowing of His love and His blessings help get us over the hurdles.

My prayer for you, Dad, as you read all this, is that your own faith will grow. Don't let this news hinder you; use it as we do: a faith-builder. God would never do anything to defeat us. The devil will, but not our Heavenly Father whose love is perfect.

We love you,
Andy, Nina and family

Postscript note: Dad was not living out an active faith when we wrote this letter to him. The good news is that within the year, he gave his heart to Jesus Christ and began seeking peace with God.

INTAKE NOTES

1. What is "unfair" in your life?

DIAGNOSTIC QUESTIONS

1. How are you, like Paul, "bound in chains" today? (Verse 7)

2. Referring to the extensive Feelings Chart in Appendix A, record here how that makes you feel.

24

PRESCRIPTION FOR FOLLOW-UP

1. In keeping with Paul's positive attitude, complete these sentences:

       I feel **PEACE**

when_____.

       I feel **JOY**

when_____.

       I am **THANKFUL**

when_____.

       I am **CONFIDENT**

in_____.

2. Who do you know that needs words of encouragement today?

3. Take five minutes right now (yes, right now) and write this person an email or send them a note letting them know they are on your heart. Tell them what you are praying for them. (Use verses 3-11 as a model.) You may even include these verses in your note, substituting the person's name where any pronouns (you, your, etc.) may be.

4. That didn't take long, did it?! Now, before jogging off to start your "to do list" for today, thank the Lord for your "positive emotions" listed in #1 of today's Prescription for Follow-Up and pray specifically for the person you listed in #2 above.

And just in case you still haven't followed up with that note of encouragement, do it right now before you get distracted!

Nina Fuller

A Dad's Journey
Brad Irwin

I had long anticipated being a father, as I did not get married until I was 27 and my wife was 36. I never really thought much about a child being born with a disability and, frankly, was more interested in the gender of the child. I wanted a son.

When we found out we were pregnant, my wife went for regular checkups and everything seemed to be fine for a while. We didn't find out the sex of the baby right away. That came at the same time we found out the baby's condition.

My wife began having complications around her sixth month of pregnancy. She had elevated blood pressure and swelling. I didn't think that much of it, naturally assuming her age would make things a bit more complicated. Our doctor ran tests on my wife, including an amniocentesis, drawing from fluid that surrounded the baby within the womb. The results came back that indicated our child would be born with Down syndrome. The doctors discussed with us how this could possibly affect the health of the child and my wife and what we should expect. Even with the "best case" scenario given to us, the picture was very grave. They presented the option of abortion to us at this time and said in so many words that it would be understandable if we chose to terminate our child's life, considering the prognosis. I was, and still am, really confused on why they presented that harsh option to us right after we were told our news. After asking them to explain, they told us it was required by federal law.

That was a lot to deal with right away. I was told I might lose my wife and my child. And, at the same time, my employment was in jeopardy due to overseas contracts.

I became depressed. I blamed myself for a lot of what was happening. When I was younger, I had used drugs and had done more than my share of drinking. I thought that now I was getting my punishment for my previous indiscretions.

In the past, I had known people who had a "retarded" child or sibling, and I knew what was said behind their backs and even publicly. I didn't want to deal with that, my pride as a man was at stake.

Our baby girl arrived, and we named her Angela. As it turns out, Angie is my reward and not my punishment. She has shown me what is important in life and helped me regain joy in living. Prior to her birth, the doctors made it sound like this child would be a burden in our lives. Nothing could be further from the truth. Our lives have definitely changed but for the better, and I am enjoying life once again.

DAILY DOSE 3

COMFORTING WORDS
II CORINTHIANS 1:3-11

"Praise be to the God and Father of our Lord Jesus Christ, the Father of compassion and the God of all comfort, who comforts us in all our troubles, so that we can comfort those in any trouble with the comfort we ourselves have received from God."

OBSERVATIONS

Here we are listening to the life-wisdom of Paul. On behalf of God the Father, Paul blesses his friends with grace and peace. He immediately turns attention to why God should be praised:

1. He is the God and Father of our Lord Jesus Christ.
2. He is the Father of compassion.
3. He is the God of all comfort.

God comforts us how? ...in ALL our troubles.

Why?...so that...we can comfort those in any trouble with the comfort we ourselves have received...From whom?...from God! Direct comfort from God to us! Personally!

Even as suffering flows into our lives, whether it be the same perils as Paul testifies about in verses 5-8, or possibly the suffering that comes from watching our child suffer, or even our own personal traumas, so, too, our comfort overflows. It all happens for a reason. Why? Our answer is found in verse 9: "so that we would not rely on ourselves but on God."

ANECDOTE

"Why would God allow this to happen to Ann and Steve?" I wondered. I had just gotten word that our friends' baby was pre-natally diagnosed with Potter's Syndrome. Matthew had been created without any kidneys. This would be fatal. No hope of survival past the womb. *Why, God?*

Matthew was born several agonizing months later. He was seemingly perfect and beautiful on the outside, as I later observed him in his tiny casket. The love that surrounded him in those hours was palpable. The Presence of a loving and compassionate Father permeated the hospital room where Matthew was born and yet destined to die within hours. That Presence, the God of all comfort, escorted Matthew's grieving family home to await their cries for comfort in their darkest hours.

Not too many years later, I received a timely note of encouragement from Matthew's mom, Ann, as I awaited the delivery and birth of my own baby. We, too, had learned in advance of our baby's birth that her life would be compromised. This innocent new life would have Down syndrome and two heart defects. We did not know if she would survive past birth.

The comfort I received from Ann was felt to the core of my being. I shuddered after reading her note, realizing she knew- **really and truly knew** – about God's comfort and was sharing that same comfort with me. It overflowed from her life to mine, reminding me of God's compassion and comfort in all our troubles. It was also the beginning of a commitment on my part to comfort others and to share our prayer concerns so that many would give thanks for the favor granted us in answer to everyone's prayers.

INTAKE NOTES

1. What troubles do you have today?

DIAGNOSTIC QUESTIONS

1. Who has recently shown you comfort?_____

2. Detail how they have comforted you:

PRESCRIPTION FOR FOLLOW-UP

1. List what you know about this person's life that has caused them to have troubles of their own.

2. Close your eyes right now, no matter what is going on around you.   Thank the Lord for the above mentioned person/people.   In spite of their own circumstances, they took time to comfort you with the same comfort they received from God. That is a comforting thought.

My Son, My Hero
Audrey Mayer

From the time I was a little girl all I ever wanted was to be a mom. Having come from a large family, I was ready to have a large family of my own.

After graduating from college, I married, and we quickly started our family. I wanted so much to have children. During each pregnancy, I did everything I could to protect my unborn child. I was just as thrilled with each life that God had placed in my care as I was with the first. We had what I considered the perfect family, two girls and two boys. I was happy, felt very blessed and thought life was perfect. I loved every aspect of being a mom and caring for my family.

God sometimes has ways of challenging us, but I have learned that through those challenges we receive blessings in ways we never thought imaginable.

When my daughter Amy was four, and I thought we were finished having babies, God blessed us once again. Timothy Wayne was born on his due date and was the easiest delivery of all. This little guy was my smallest baby weighing in at five pounds even. My other children had birth weights ranging from 8.5 pounds to 9.5 pounds, so when Tim failed to grow and thrive I assumed that he was just so small and needed to catch up.

Around Tim's six month checkup, the doctor stated that Timmy was really behind and he wanted him to see some specialists. I remember listening to the doctor tell me all the different things that it might be. He ended his sentence saying, "At the worst, your son may have cerebral palsy." I was numb as we drove home that day, it was so surreal.

These things did not happen to people like me, I said to myself. I take good care of my children. I have always had good medical care with my pregnancies. I love my babies. In my thinking, things like this only happen to women that don't

31

care, so why did this happen to me. I was angry, confused and felt very alone.

At nine months, my son was diagnosed with cerebral palsy. I immediately got him into an early intervention program. We went daily to a center to get services. Timmy had physical, occupational and speech therapy every day of the week. I was determined to "fix" him. I just knew that if he had enough therapies he would get "well," and my son would be normal.

After a year of exhausting trips for therapy, we went back to the CP clinic for an evaluation and update. This clinic visit was heartbreaking; after all we had been through, Tim had made very little progress. I was told that the normal life expectancy for children with my son's brain abnormality was 24 months. I was stunned, numb and angry. Life expectancy-- what was all this about? Mothers are not supposed to hear about their child's life expectancy; my son should have to bury me, not the other way around.

After that visit, I fell into a deep pit of despair. I lost all my hope; I wanted more than life itself for my son to be healthy and strong. I grieved deeply for the son I lost, the son of my dreams. I escaped the world by locking myself up in my room.

I cried from the depth of my soul for God to heal my son. I bargained with God; I was a desperate mother pleading for her son. God had lost a Son. He knew my grief and that gave me such comfort. I wanted my son to live and know life and happiness. I wanted him to run and wear out shoes and talk his head off. Little did I know that God was hearing my cries and would answer.

A few weeks later we were in the car again heading to therapy. Timmy was riding in the front seat in his car seat. I was lost in my thoughts, having a real pity party for myself. Suddenly, Timmy started pounding on his car seat, trying to get my attention. He was two and had quite a charming smile. He was holding up his crooked little finger and moving it in a circle. I looked at him and smiled and said, "Yes, Timmy, I see your finger." He continued yelling in his Timmy babble and circling his little crooked finger. It was then I realized he wanted me to sing with him....his favorite song..."This Little Light of Mine." I sang, and Timmy smiled and did all the motions.

God opened my shortsighted eyes that day, and for the first time I saw my son the way God does. He is a beautiful, perfect light, and he does shine. Tim shine's everywhere he goes. He has a smile that will knock your socks off and a sense of humor that keeps everyone in stitches. He is so loving and has an innocence that is so precious.

Timmy has become "Tim." He is now a teenager. He does not wear out tennis shoes but does wear out tires on his power wheelchair. He talks with the aid of a laptop and has even been sent to the office for talking too much at school!

In Jeremiah 1:5, we read, "Before I formed you in the womb I knew you, before you were born I set you apart." God knew my son before he was born. He KNEW Tim when his brain did not form completely at 24 weeks' gestation, and yet he chose for him to live. God KNEW at birth that there would be complications, yet He CHOSE life for Tim. I find great comfort that my God knew the plan He had for Tim in spite of everything the world deems crippled. My son is my hero; he has taught me to look at life in a totally different way, knowing how fragile and precious every day is. He has taught me to be far more accepting of others, and everyday he teaches me more about patience.

DAILY DOSE 4

STAGGERING
PROVERBS 3:5-8

"Trust in the Lord with all your heart and lean not on your own understanding; in all your ways acknowledge him, and he will make your paths straight."

OBSERVATIONS

Familiar to many believers, this powerful passage of God's Word holds six commands (and you thought there were just those other ten) and the resulting promises. Let's take a look at today's spiritual therapy:

Through the wisdom of King Solomon, absolutely the wisest man on earth, (refer to I Kings 3; II Chronicles 1 for more info) we are given these commands:

1. Trust in the Lord - not any man or woman or circumstance.

Parenthetical question- How much are you commanded to trust Him?
Literal answer: With **ALL** your heart – not just a portion.

2. Do not lean on your own understanding – ("Who, me, God?")

3. In ALL your ways acknowledge the Lord – surrender every aspect of your life to Him

The result of obeying these commands is the following promise:

He (the Lord) will make straight your twisted path.

The next installment of commands that precede God's ensuing promise in this passage:

4. Do not be wise in your own eyes – Don't take matters into your own hands.

5. Fear the Lord – Yes, you!

6. Shun evil – This, too, is an indisputable command, not a passive suggestion.

The resulting promise: good health for your body and nourishment for your bones. In our quest for spiritual therapy, these premises are promises of good physical health!

ANECDOTE

As I staggered down each step and through the hallway leading to my pastor's study, the doctor's words delivered less than an hour before pounded in my head. "The baby girl you are carrying has Tri-somy 21, confirmed by the amniocentesis we have received." The words pulsated through my brain, causing me to be nauseated and dizzy as I tried to maintain my composure and balance as I reeled through the church. I could hardly put one foot in front of the other. If they hadn't known better, the church staff would have suspected that I was inebriated. I leaned on my husband, Andy, to hold me up, yet he, too, was dealing with his own shock and grief.

We couldn't believe this was happening to us – good Christian people who simply wanted one more baby to love after having three boys. I always loved being pregnant, feeling new life growing inside of my body, partnering with God in the miracle of new birth, and looking forward to the wonder-filled bond of nursing my babies. That's what I wanted to happen with this fourth baby. My understanding of what motherhood was all about was brutally being abducted. My perceptions and knowledge were under siege with this most recent assault on my walk with God. I knew that my path felt awfully crooked, scattered with debris of doubt, fear, anger, regret and sorrow.

I remembered this passage and its commands, beginning with the all-powerful reminder to "Trust in the Lord" with every fiber of my being. Then, there was the gentle but assertive command reminding me not to lean on any previous knowledge of my own. *How did God know that I would be prone to do that, anyway?!*

Using Solomon's wisdom put to paper, the Lord commanded me to acknowledge Him and recognize His divine Hand in every detail of my life, including this pre-born child. The result of my obedience to God would be that He would make my crooked, staggering path straight. If I followed His commands, He promised to straighten out what seemingly had become the worst event of my life.

INTAKE NOTES

1. What ails you physically today?

2. What emotions are you feeling today? (Refer to the Feelings Chart, Appendix A)

3. Do you feel the path you are on today is crooked?

4. What debris do you see? (What clutters your path?)

5. We are commanded to not be wise in our own eyes, to fear the Lord and to shun evil (verse 7). The foolish wisdom from the world's view tells pre-natally diagnosed women to "abort/terminate," as their first option. Do you see this as an "evil to shun?"

6. The ability we have to shun evil comes how? (See verse 7) _____the Lord and (by doing so, you will) shun evil.

DIAGNOSTIC QUESTIONS

1. What were some of your presumptions (your own understanding) of handicapped children prior to having your own?

2. What understanding has God taught you through your special needs child that you would not have learned by walking a totally different path?

PRESCRIPTION FOR FOLLOW-UP

Stop in your tracks right now, no matter what your path looks like today. Acknowledge God's presence (pray) and thank Him for the new understanding He has given you (using your answers from Diagnostic Question #2) on this path you are taking into the special needs world.

Loving Lauren
Becky Mischler

After losing my first daughter to a stillbirth, I ached to hold another baby of my own. One year later, we found out we were expecting again. Answering our prayers, God kept me healthy and strong throughout this new pregnancy. On November 9, 1992, Lauren Brianne was born. Lauren had even more dark hair than Kaylin. Her tiny fingers and toes were delightfully moving all over and she had a great set of lungs! Joe and I cried tears of joy and relief as Lauren wailed at the top of her lungs. She was given a top Apgar score, and we were thanking the Lord for a safe delivery of a healthy baby.

In the first few days home, I was concerned Lauren slept so much. I contacted the pediatrician. He assured me it was okay, explaining some babies sleep more than others. By the end of the first week, I called the doctor again. I noticed every time Lauren was feeding, she would gag. Her eyes rolled to the right and her right side would tremor. She was still sleeping way too long. The only time Lauren was awake was during feeding. At this point, the doctor had me bring the baby in right away. While we were there, Lauren had one of her episodes. The doctor was concerned Lauren might be having seizures. This would explain why she was sleeping so much. He ordered immediate tests. The EEG confirmed the seizures and the MRI and CAT scans showed Lauren had Schizencephaly, complete Agenisis of the Corpus Callosum and many areas of the Cortical Dysplasia. The neurologist could not tell us what to expect regarding Lauren's future development. We were told she may never walk or talk. They told us some children with this diagnosis have feeding tubes their entire lives. The developmental range was so broad that the doctors said we would just have to wait and see how Lauren developed over the years.

It was hard to believe what we were being told. Lauren looked just like any typical infant with no abnormal physical attributes. I wanted to know what I needed to do for Lauren. How was I going to take care of her? *Could* I take care of her? We felt isolated. We constantly asked God to give us strength and courage to take care of Lauren.

Joe and I felt it would be in Lauren's best interest if I quit work and stayed home with her. We were accustomed to living on two incomes and we knew there would be extra sacrifices, but we also knew that Lauren's needs were top priority.

Not working out of the home ended up being one of the best things I've ever done for both of our children. Our son, Brian, was at a critical age and needed as much of our attention as Lauren. We didn't want him to feel pushed aside. We always made sure he did not have to miss out on activities he enjoyed and Joe and I stayed involved in Brian's activities with him. We made sure to make time for him around all of Lauren's therapies, doctor appointments, emergency room visits and hospital stays.

DAILY DOSE 5

WHO'S TO BLAME?
JOHN 9:1-3

"As he went along, he saw a man blind from birth. His disciples asked him, 'Rabbi, who sinned, this man or his parents, that he was born blind?' 'Neither this man nor his parents sinned,' said Jesus, 'but this happened so that the work of God might be displayed in his life.'"

Jesus was strolling along with his vagabond group of disciples one day. Knowing their predisposition to the culture's prejudices, Jesus used a man with special needs to teach His followers a dynamic lesson, perhaps the very purpose for which the man was born. Think about it: God is still using this mysterious, unnamed man to teach us lessons almost 2,000 years later. Let's jump in step with the traveling disciples...

OBSERVATIONS

Verse 1 - Being God, Jesus already knew their smug attitudes but let them verbalize their faulty thinking.

Verse 2 - Acknowledging Jesus as their teacher (Rabbi) the disciples asked him a question based on a teaching of the culture that handicaps were a result of someone's sins. Their thinking was, "if someone had not sinned, then the man would not be punished with blindness."

Verse 3 - Jesus' reply was assertive and humbling: "Neither this man nor his parents sinned"! We can almost hear the disciples' chatter as they imagined who else could be blamed for this "tragedy" of blindness. There was only one other conclusion of who was to blame, and Jesus knew what the new believers were thinking but they dared not utter. God was responsible for this man's darkness of sight, his parents' shame and his pitiful beggar's life. Jesus interrupted not only their walk along the way, but He revealed to his disciples a new path of thinking. The man's blindness was not a result of anyone's sin, but it was intentional, purposeful and valuable. He was created blind **so that** the work of God might be displayed in his life.

ANECDOTE

The package arrived in the mail that chilly December afternoon, and I didn't recognize the handwriting. There was no return address. "Oh," I thought, "We have a secret Santa; how nice." Once I opened the package, I discovered a cassette tape and photo copies of several articles on faith-healing. An anonymous note told me, "If you confess all your sins, pray hard enough, and believe with all your heart that the baby you are carrying will be cured from Down syndrome, God will heal her."

Shortly before we tossed the well-meaning but totally offensive (and faulty) material in the wastebasket, my husband and I took comfort in the truth that the Creator of this tiny life growing inside me had specific biological rules in place. Most people are born with 23 pairs of chromosomes in every cell of their bodies, for a total of 46. A person with Down syndrome has 47 chromosomes. The extra chromosome is always the 21st chromosome. Whenever there is too much or too little genetic information, growth and development are affected.

This pre-born baby girl growing inside my womb was being formed by God just the way He wanted her to be created, extra chromosome and all. It was not my place to try to manipulate God with a contrived prayer.

We knew that we were to faithfully trust God whatever His Will, and not try to outwit God to make Him do *our* will. We would rest in His Sovereignty, knowing the only sin we would be committing was the sin of disobedience if we took matters into our own hands.

Today, the work of God is being displayed in the life of our wonderful little girl, and we are convinced that she will be used by Him for years to come to.

INTAKE NOTES

1. Has anyone (maybe even yourself) blamed you for your child's disability?

2. What did they say to you?

DIAGNOSTIC QUESTIONS

What emotions are you feeling as you think about those conversations? (Refer to Appendix A)

PRESCRIPTION FOR FOLLOW-UP

1. Knowing the truth after reading today's Daily Dose of therapy, (your child's disability has happened **so that** the work of God might be displayed), list ways that your child and your family are displaying the work of God to others:
   1.

   2.

   3.

2. Take a walk with the Lord today, even if it's going to another room in your house. Thank Him for reminding you of His truth which negates others' faulty thinking. Offer up to God any faulty thinking of your own and receive His unconditional love today. Be sure to thank God for choosing your child and your family to intentionally carry out His work.

BELLA'S STORY
Deidre Pujols

When I was 16 years old, I walked the aisle at church to get "born again," but it was not until I was 20 years old, pregnant and by myself that I truly understood what becoming a Christian meant. I realized that being pregnant was going to change everything in my life, and being alone did not make it any easier. I lived with my mom and dad at the time, so they really supported me through the entire nine months.

The young man I had been involved with, the baby's father, was in Boston and I had just moved back to Kansas City after living in Boston for a year. He had offered to fly me back to Boston to get an abortion, and I told him he was crazy and that was that.

Being pregnant really brought me to my knees, and I had such a desire to know God and get my life right with Him.

On November 26, 1997, even before the doctors had a chance to do a chromosome test on newborn Baby Isabella, I knew she had Down syndrome. For me, it was my first encounter with God Himself! He told me she had Down syndrome the moment she was laid on my chest. It was a situation that is so hard to put into words.

It was such an emotional time when my mom and dad realized what I already knew. Isabella had Down syndrome. We all cried. We could not understand how a day to be celebrated was like the day of a death.

Even in all the confusion and tears, deep within me I knew it was going to be alright. When I was trying to fathom all that was happening, my mom made the nurse at the hospital roll Isabella back into the room. I remember seeing Bella all bundled up with a little hat on her tiny head. I took one look at her and was never so in love in all my life as I was with my baby girl. She was so innocent and sweet. All I could do was hold her and cry.

I had the name "Isabella" picked out before she was born. I actually had a brief moment thinking I should name her something different because now she wasn't going to be my perfect little girl with the perfect name. How silly was that idea?

I went through a gamut of emotions. At one point, I was embarrassed to tell people about Bella's Down syndrome, thinking it somehow was a reflection on me or something I had done.

There was also the time I called my best friend, crying, and told her how I wish God would just take Bella back because I felt so bad about how she was going to live. There are so many thoughts and feelings you experience during a time such as this, but nothing is more powerful than completely trusting God for every detail of the future. I knew He came to my bedside the morning Bella was born, and He brought me the peace I needed to deal with what followed.

A couple of months after Bella was born, I met the man who would soon be my husband. Albert has been an angel from day one, and he has become a father to Bella. Thanks to having a career now in major league baseball, we have a platform from the Lord to help bring awareness about Down syndrome to others. Our family is approached by so many people who also have a loved one with Down syndrome, and we cheer them on to keep fighting the good fight. I encourage them to get informed about Down syndrome because information is power. There is also power in numbers. We encourage people to get connected to their local Down syndrome association and enjoy celebrating life.

Bella has been our inspiration in so many ways, including establishing the Pujols Family Foundation. At the core of the Pujols Family Foundation is the belief that every person is special in the sight of God. We are committed to a calling of love and service, dedicating our lives to seeing every child as God's creation – more precious and important to Him than anyone could ever imagine. We are dedicated to the love, care and development of people with Down syndrome and their families. The Pujols Family Foundation also has a global vision reaching out to impoverished families and children in the Dominican Republic, Albert's native country.

We have each been blessed with different talents and abilities that come together to create a team that is greater than the sum of its parts. God has an intentional plan for each life and places each of us exactly where we are supposed to be.

It has been eight years since Isabella was born, and the mystery is gone. God clearly had taken something originated from my sin and a careless lifestyle and made it something wonderful. His love has been made abundantly clear in our lives through Bella.

GOD IS PRO-CHOICE
DEUTERONOMY 30:11-20

"Now what I am commanding you today is not too difficult for you or beyond your reach. It is not up in heaven, so that you have to ask, 'Who will ascend into heaven to get it and proclaim it to us so we may obey it?' Nor, is it beyond the sea, so that you have to ask, 'Who will cross the sea to get it and proclaim it to us so we may obey it?' No, the word is very near you; it is in your mouth and in your heart so you may obey it.

"See, I set before you today life and prosperity, death and destruction. For I command you today to love the Lord your God, to walk in his ways, and to keep his commands, decrees and laws; then you will live and increase, and the Lord your God will bless you in the land you are entering to possess. But if your heart turns away and you are not obedient, and if you are drawn away to bow down to other gods and worship them, I declare to you this day that you will certainly be destroyed. You will not live long in the land you are crossing the Jordan to enter and possess. This day I call heaven and earth as witnesses again you that I have set before you life and death, blessings and curses. Now choose life, so that you and your children may live and that you may love the Lord your God, listen to his voice, and hold fast to him. For the Lord is your life and He will give you many years in the land He swore to give your fathers, Abraham, Isaac and Jacob."

OBSERVATIONS

There are no excuses for not knowing what God's Will is for us on the subject of being "pro-life" or "pro-choice" as American politics has coined this issue. God is pro-choice; ever hear of "Free Will"? He just wants us all to choose wisely on the side of life!

Verses 11-13 are clear: We cannot claim that His command is too difficult or too lofty to obey. We dare not say, "but...but...but, you don't understand what I am going through. I have no options...."

As if God, Himself, is having a direct conversation with us, we hear these words of rebuttal from Him. Take a look at verses 14-16:

> "No, the word is very near you – ...in your heart so you may obey it... Now choose life so that you and your children may live..."

Consequently, by making the right choice (to choose life) when the time comes, we will be able to:

- Live – both parents and children.
- Love the Lord.
- Listen to His Voice.
- Hold fast to Him.

Why? "Because the Lord **IS** our life and it is He who will reward us with many years..."

ANECDOTE

Everything was out of control and only God knew if our unborn baby and I would survive my congestive heart failure, kidney failure and pulmonary edema that threatened both our lives.

"God, am I supposed to give up my life for this baby who might not survive anyway? Would she have to die so I could survive this physical assault on my body? My times are in Your hands, God, and I trust You with our lives."

Throughout this complicated pregnancy, we chose life for our compromised baby. We chose life instead of abortion when the baby was pre-natally diagnosed with a severe disability. We chose life when the baby was also diagnosed with two heart defects. We chose life when the pregnancy thrust me into severe panic attacks and annoying phobias. We chose life the night of February 10th during my seventh month of pregnancy when the doctor declared that the pregnancy must be terminated immediately to save my life.

Knowing that I faced losing my life here on earth, I silently soaked in the vision of my youngest son from across the room. "I love you, Joey," I whispered under my breath as I clung to my husband's hand and to my very life.

Two and a half days later, I awakened to learn that both my 2 pound 11 ounce baby girl and I were alive! God's Word rang clear and true like never before. *"Choose life so that you and your children may live."* We are living out the rest of that passage as we love the Lord, listen to His voice and hold fast to Him each day.

INTAKE NOTES

1. Have you been close to death because of a pregnancy? If not, have you loved someone else who has been close to death because of their pregnancy?

DIAGNOSTIC QUESTIONS

1. What emotions reeled through your spirit during that time?

2. What got you through that time?

PRESCRIPTION FOR FOLLOW-UP

1. List 3 character qualities of God that you saw up close during that life threatening crisis:
   1.
   2.
   3.

2. Thank God for sparing your life (or your loved one). Ask Him to reveal to you how He wants to use you while you are still this side of eternity. Listen to His voice and write down what He reveals to you.

Nina Fuller

Doing the Right Thing

Mindy George

During my second pregnancy I had a blood test to determine if I would have a child with a birth defect. Five days later, my physician called with news that my levels were elevated. These tests, however, were not always accurate. She wanted me to go for further testing and informed me that my baby could potentially have a neural tube defect, ranging from anencephaly to spina bifida. Ten days later, after much praying for the best possible outcome, we were told that our son had spina bifida. We were immediately given three options: abortion, experimental surgery or continue the pregnancy as is. My husband and I knew that we would continue the pregnancy and after some research decided not to have experimental surgery. During the next few months, we received several opinions from family and friends regarding our decision, not all in our favor, but we knew we were doing the right thing.

After many months of prayer, worry and anxiety, my son, Owen, was born in February 2000. He looked just like any other newborn except for the opening in his back. The next day he had surgery to close his back and insert a shunt to control the hydrocephalus. This surgery was the beginning of several surgeries, therapies, doctor appointments and emergency room visits.

Through all of it, I continue to learn how precious life is. Both of my kids have taught me how life's downs are also accompanied by many more ups. Sometimes you have to look a little harder for them, but they are there. Owen's first steps walking with a walker are just as important as my daughter's first steps walking independently.

One of the most difficult things lately has been trying to explain to Owen why he has to use canes and whether he will have another surgery. I don't think he understands just yet (he is only five), but I will continue to explain it to him the best I can.

Owen is one of the happiest kids I know. He is always smiling and laughing and can warm anybody's heart. God entrusted him to my husband and me; therefore, I have to trust God in His decision that we are doing the right thing. There are several days and nights that I pray, asking God to let Owen not need any more surgeries or tests done. There are just as many nights that I thank him for how far Owen has come. I thank him for letting Owen walk with canes, for starting Kindergarten with "regular" classmates and for allowing him to be as happy as he is.

This is the first year that we do not have a potential surgery looming. It has been wonderful, but at the same time, I am waiting for something to happen. I always seem to have in the back of my mind the "what ifs" and what should we do if he gets sick, hurt, etc. I try to let Owen do all he can to be a regular kid. There are many opportunities in the community for him to participate, like taking Taekwondo. I have to have faith that if Owen can find a way to participate, he will be okay. He needs to be allowed to enjoy everyday life like other boys his age.

Because of my son, I have realized that all of us have different abilities. We all need help in some areas, and we each have strengths to celebrate.

DAILY DOSE 7

WILD HORSES AND WILD THOUGHTS
II CORINTHIANS 10:3-5

"For though we live in the world, we do not wage war as the world does. The weapons we fight with are not the weapons of the world. On the contrary, they have divine power to demolish strongholds. We demolish arguments and every pretension that sets itself up against the knowledge of God, and we take captive every thought to make it obedient to Christ."

OBSERVATIONS

Let's take a look at this vaguely familiar passage of scripture in light of those who face a crisis pregnancy:

Verse 3 – Even though we live in the world, we are not to deal with issues like the world does:

- Abortion is one, if not *the* most threatening issue in the world today because it destroys innocent human life that God created.

- Abortion is the world's way of dealing with a crisis pregnancy.

Verse 4 - The weapons we use to fight our battles are not those of fear or manipulation or lies. The weapons we DO possess (see Ephesians 6:10-20) have divine power to demolish strongholds.

What are some of the strongholds?

1. Fear of the handicapped.
2. Increased financial needs.
3. Worry about others' rejection and misjudgments,
4. Fear of how *this* baby will affect our other children.
5. Losing our own life.

Verse 5 – We demolish arguments and *every* pretension that sets itself up against the knowledge of God.

What are some of those pretensions/arguments (i.e., lies):

1. Pregnancy is a "product of conception."
2. It's not a baby, it's a "fetus."
3. A woman has the "right" to choose....to murder.
4. Abortion is legal – Roe v Wade (1972) is based on a lie.
5. Mother's life is more valuable than a fetus'.
6. Handicapped baby won't have any quality of life and will be a burden.

Verse 5 – We take captive *every thought* to make it obedient to Christ.

Like wild horses that stampede, what are some of the wild thoughts that need to be reigned in and controlled during our times of feeling out of control:

1. What will this child look like?
2. Will this baby be rejected and not loved by others?
3. Am I capable of really meeting his/her every need?
4. Life will be a constant struggle.
5. What if the baby dies anyway after all we go through?

ANECDOTE:

We gathered our three rambunctious sons to share the somber news with them. Earlier that day, Andy and I received news about our unborn baby that would change our family forever. Our sons had been excited four months earlier to learn we would be adding a new baby to our family! We would be welcoming a long-desired baby sister into our brood of boys. I was elated to finally get to shop for pink ruffles and pretty frills instead of baseball blue and fire engine red!

However, we were reeling from the bleak news that our doctor gently confirmed after testing: *the baby you are carrying will have Down syndrome and two heart defects.* How would we share this devastating news with our sons? How would this tragedy affect our boys' future? Would the baby even die before birth? We had no answers and felt powerless as we presented ourselves to our children.

As we told Jesse, Jake, and Joey that their baby sister would be born with these special needs, we told them we didn't know what God was doing, but we would trust Him for the baby and for each of us. He had created this baby for a purpose, and we would go through this together. Andy asked us to all bow our heads, close our eyes and we were going to pray. Typically, each time we prayed as a family, one brother or another would try to make the others giggle and consequently get scolded for their inappropriate behavior. This particular time of prayer held complete sobriety. After asking God to protect and take care of all our needs through this trial, we said "Amen." Immediately, Jesse spoke up, "Mom! Dad! I know why God is giving **us** this baby. It's so **we** won't abort her!"

We were amazed at this 13 year old boy's personal ownership of my pregnancy. Jesse would never be pregnant! He would never know what it was like to have the sensation of new life pushing and moving and growing inside of his body. Yet, he had taken on my pregnancy for himself. I was not the sole proprietor of this baby's life. This baby belonged to her daddy, her three big brothers who already loved her, and to a world waiting for her arrival. My adolescent son understood that part of the answer to "Why us, God" was that **we** valued human life at every level, and we would not take matters into our own hands as the world does. We would not abort this innocent baby even though by the law of the land we had every right. Jesse was learning that we adhered to a law much greater than civil law. We obeyed God, the Supreme Judge of the universe. God had confidence in the Fuller family and we, Andy, Nina, Jesse, Jake and Joey would not destroy the life of this new little family member! God trusted us to protect her, and we would trust Him to take care of all of us.

INTAKE NOTES

1. Have you ever read today's passage of Scripture in this context? I recommend you highlight it in your Bible.

2. If you have teenage/adult children, do you know what they believe regarding abortion?

DIAGNOSTIC QUESTIONS

1. How do **you** manage to control any raging thoughts that cause you panic?

PRESCRIPTION FOR FOLLOW-UP

1. Take a look at the following Scriptures and truth:
   1. God is the Creator of each life – Psalm 139:13-16
   2. God has a Plan for each life – Jeremiah 1:4-5, Jeremiah 29:11
   3. God will make a way for each of us – Proverbs 3:5, 6

2. Like wild horses, we can reign in our wild thoughts by clinging to the absolute truths of God's Word. Work on memorizing the above passages.

3. On a postcard, write and keep handy these thoughts:
   KNOW GOD'S WORD
   TRUST GOD'S WORD
   OBEY GOD'S WORD

Nina Fuller

A Dragon Not Slain

Anonymous

"Mom – Mom! It's terrible! I saw him!" Our son crashed through the front door and collapsed into my arms as I sat in my easy chair. "He killed her! I saw him," he repeated.

From the look of horror on his face, I could tell whatever he thought he saw extremely traumatized him.

"Who? Who did you see kill someone?"

"Mr. Danfield! He killed his wife! I saw him through the window." I could feel his body tremble in panic and his snotty nose ran down and over his lips. I grimaced at my arthritic shoulder as his grip on me became more desperate.

He was diagnosed at birth with Ring Chromosome 8, and the doctors painted a very dark picture for our son's future. It was a shock to our family. They actually predicted he would not be able to attend school... but the Lord had another idea.

Adam (not his real name) suffered a mild dysfunction of his brain. As it turned out, he could read as well as most but could not grasp mathematical concepts or values, so the special education classes in the school system were a good fit for him. He was a happy-go-lucky little fellow, and most people loved and accepted him as he was, even though there were physical deformities that suggested a handicap.

It is interesting, however, that even though this was a significant handicap, God gave Adam a very great gift - that of understanding scripture. Many times, he has blessed us and others with this undeniable and amazing gift. He is able to pray for people with discernment of their needs as well.

In his teens, however, and after the delusional incident of the murder, my husband and I sought answers from Adam's doctors at the University of Washington.

This was their diagnosis: "We have discovered that often, a patient who has anything wrong with the eighth chromosome may develop schizophrenia." The doctor scanned Adam's chart. "With the delusions, paranoia and depression, our team of doctors has diagnosed him with what is called Schizo Affective Disorder."

Dumbfounded, we sat there, stunned. "Why, God? Why did our son receive a second blow like this? God had helped our family through so many adjustments to our lives because of Adam's problems. Yet, every problem seemed to be met with good answers, not answers that would change what he was, but answers that would allow us to cope. But--schizophrenia?

The great encourager, my husband, put his arms around me. "Honey, we handled the first battle, we'll handle this new one, too."

Schizophrenia, however, is a dragon not slain. Heavy medications, obsessive compulsive disorders, delusions and a life of fear and agony beset our son. It broke our hearts. We have seen most of his dreams come and go. It is true sadness.

While we sometimes lost our son to some deep, dark place we can only imagine, now medications stabilize him. Left far behind, however, is the energetic, fun-loving son, overcome by one who lives a numbing lifestyle.

Early on, I became paralyzed by the thought that we might have to institutionalize our son because of growing problems we were unable to handle. "The idea terrifies me," I cried on my husband's shoulder. Yet, God's provision greeted me during my morning scripture reading:

Joshua 1:9: *"Be strong and courageous.* <u>*Do not be terrified:*</u> <u>*Do not be discouraged,*</u> *for the Lord your God will be with you wherever you go."*

My husband and I are guilty of trying to handle the problems with our son all in our own strength, but we don't have enough strength anymore. It takes the support of our entire family to deal with this illness. I don't know what is ahead for our son, but I know God is telling us not to be afraid or discouraged because He is with us in all circumstances.

It is such encouragement to know that we can rely on God's strength, and that He will never let us down. He will meet us in all circumstances. We may never receive the miracle healing we pray for, but we will surely receive everything we need to sustain us in each and every situation.

Isn't God good!! Amen

DAILY DOSE 8

THE SECRET'S OUT
Esther 4:14

"For if you remain silent at this time, relief and deliverance for the Jews will arise from another place, but you and your father's family will perish. And who knows but that you have come to a royal position for such a time as this?"

OBSERVATIONS

Prior to becoming the new "Mrs. Xerxes, Queen of the Royal Kingdom," Esther was a young Jewish orphan, adopted by her cousin who insisted they keep her heritage private. Her life was already shadowed by loss, grief, sorrow and secrets. The Lord was going to use her life to make a difference. Here are some historical, biblical facts about Esther's situation:

1. 1:1-12 - The pagan king, Xerxes, was temperamental, among other things.
2. 2:1-9 - Xerxes invested a lot of effort and money in his search for a replacement queen.
3. 2:10 - Esther had a lifetime secret that remained undisclosed.
4. 2:17 - Esther was the beauty contest winner and was crowned Queen.
5. 2:19-23 - Both Esther and Mordecai, her cousin, found favor with the king when they helped save his life from a plot against him.

6. 3:1-4:8 -The evil Haman convinced the King to decree death upon all Jews which would unwittingly include his beautiful queen
7. 4:8 - Esther realized she had been placed in her position of influence for this exact time in her life.
8. 4:15 - Esther knew she could lose her life one way or another, and she asked for prayer from others to help her carry out God's calling on her life.
9. 4:16-9:30 - In spite of her fears, Esther forged ahead, sought God's wisdom and leading.
10. 4:16-9:30 - Not only was Esther's life spared, but also those of an entire nation of people who would have been put to death if not for her decision to get involved.

ANECDOTE

There were 20,000 women sitting in the audience that day but I felt like I was the only one present in the moment. The speaker at this *Renewing the Heart* conference had just posed a question to us. "Like Esther, what has God allowed to happen in your life that you could be used to help save His people? You have been born for such a time as this. What could it be?"

As I pondered my rhetorical answer, the room seemed to go dark, the thousands of other women were seemingly silent, and a penumbra, a heavenly glow, took over. God had just spoken to me! I had been praying throughout this conference for God to give me direction about pursuing a speaking career. I had been occasionally sharing my personal crisis pregnancy story at various gatherings and felt like I needed to do more. My goal in attending this conference was to discern God's voice as I sought Him for my next step in His calling on my life.

"What life experience have you personally endured that you can be used by God to help save lives like Queen Esther did?" the pretty blonde speaker challenged.

I knew God was beckoning me to become publicly open about my pro-life beliefs. I could help save the lives of the unborn of our nation. If we trust God and obey His Word, He will bless us and give our live experiences purpose.

"If I perish, I perish" was the resolve of Queen Esther once she knew her purpose in life was to do her best to help save God's people. God did not require her life at that time, and He used this woman of faith in dynamic ways. That is my heart's desire, as well.

INTAKE NOTES

1. Using the **Feelings Chart in Appendix A**, record here the words that best describe how you are feeling today:

2. Which of your own life experiences came to mind as you read today's Anecdote:
   1.
   2.
   3.

DIAGNOSTIC QUESTIONS

1. It is not by coincidence that your life is the way it is right now. What is YOUR answer to the question "How can God use you to help save His people?"

PRESCRIPTION FOR FOLLOW-UP

1. List 3-5 friends you can enlist to pray for you regularly as you seek God's purpose:

   Name   **Phone #**   **Email**

2. Call and ask each of these friends to partner in prayer with you. Update them often on prayer needs and praise reports.

Forever Changed

Marcia Jones

"Here, let me weigh your baby." The nurse said and took him from me. It was with those simple words that the nightmare started. When Andrew was almost five months old, over a long weekend, he went from a large, robust, happy baby, able to bounce on my legs and peek over my shoulder to a "floppy kid"--moaning and unable to eat, hold toys, sit or stand. The doctors at our pediatric office took one look at him and told me to meet them at the hospital. They had no idea what was wrong with our son but could see the loss of muscle control and inability to feed that was leading to dehydration. He had already lost two pounds from his previous visit, two weeks before when he weighed 19 pounds and was 28 inches long.

In 1973, even though my husband was a junior in medical school, and I was a Registered Nurse, as parents, we were never allowed to stay in the hospital with Andrew during this illness. The hospital held to a policy that the child would form a mistrust of the parents, assuming his parents were allowing many painful procedures to happen to him. Since Drew was a nursing infant, this was a devastating policy. In addition, we discovered later that Drew experienced several medical errors by doctors, medical students and residents attending him. During his hospitalization he suffered two cardiac/respiratory arrests, the second one for over 20 minutes, resulting in profound brain damage. Those medical errors would not have occurred under a mother's watchful eye. We were told on three separate occasions to prepare for his imminent death. During 51 days of hospitalization, our lives were forever changed.

At 15 months of age, Andrew started having a very high fever, his head became swollen and his eyes bulged. He was again hospitalized and was diagnosed with a brain abscess. If he had been a normal healthy toddler, surgery would have been performed after antibiotic therapy to remove the abscess. Due to the previous brain damage, no treatment was performed and he was sent home to die. Two weeks later, he went into a coma but managed to pull through again. Drew lived to be 20 and a half years old. He had definite periods of being awake and asleep but would probably be classified, much as in the case of Terry Shiavo -- living in a persistent vegetative state. He suffered from several types of seizure

59

activity and was classified as a child with cerebral palsy for the rest of his life. He suffered many of the routine childhood illnesses such as chickenpox, but Drew seemed to always develop secondary infections and problems. He avoided a feeding tube until he was 16 years old, when his esophagus started to ulcerate and bleed, making a gastrostomy tube necessary.

We had four children total in our family: David, Andrew, Timothy and Julie Rebecca. Life with a severely disabled child is difficult but not impossible. Since Drew burned badly in the sun, disliked his wheelchair, showed very little interest in his surroundings and suffered increased seizure activity with the heat, any vacations, other than visiting grandparents, were not acceptable for him. The only way to take a family bike ride or outing was if someone stayed at home or we hired a babysitter. Even taking Drew to the movies, shopping or anywhere in the '70s and '80s was a challenge. The term "wheelchair accessibility" had not been addressed as it is today in the 21st century. We found great babysitters through our friends at church, nursing students and Drew's school bus drivers.

Andrew attended a little preschool from the age of 30 months old until age five. The Public School Act #138 started in our community just in time for him to start school at age six. This allowed the rest of us to carry on with the regular activities of work for Dad, school for siblings and housework, Bible study and fellowship with friends for Mom. Because of Drew's fragile health and lack of outside services at the time, I chose not to work outside of the home.

In the early fall of 1973, just before Drew became ill, I turned to my husband one night and told him that I truly wanted God to be number one in my life, not really caring what it took for that to happen. I have often wondered if our enemy Satan didn't eaves drop on that prayer and, much as the book of Job illustrates, let us have it. Through it all, we saw God teach and provide for us in many ways. I learned that one of the secrets to life is learning an attitude of gratitude, to look for the praiseworthy things to focus on instead of the negative. Drew's hospital bill was paid for completely, and that was a praiseworthy thing as we could not pay that huge debt as students. We did not sue anyone for the malpractice done to Drew. Lawsuits were left to the rich and famous not the struggling medical student in the '70s.

We drew closer as a family. Grandparents, aunts, uncles and cousins, as well as the communities they all lived in, prayed for Drew. Several family members were drawn closer to Christ in praying for Drew. Our three other children would pray, along with their father and me, for Andrew to be healed: "get up, run around and play." He was taken to Kathryn Kuhlman and several other faith healers, always hoping for a miraculous healing.

Many people prayed persistently for Drew's healing, but that's just not what God had planned. This hurt all of us, for we all tend to think, "If God really loves me, He would heal those we love so very much." I will have to say that it was a full 20 years of questioning God's love for me, studying the Bible and trying to figure God out. Most of the time, I felt punished, depressed and angry.

After Andrew died, a counselor told me that I had lived most of the past 20 years in "survivor mode" - doing whatever necessary to perform and live up to others' expectations of me.

It has indeed taken several years of further Bible study and wise Christian counsel to see that Jesus really does loves me unconditionally, that He did die for me and was not punishing me for anything. Jesus is not a good luck charm or a cosmic Santa Claus. His ways are not our ways (Isaiah 55:8-9), and His agenda is all about changing our selfish, sinful personalities into His own image (Romans 8:28-29). How wise we would all be to cooperate with His higher plan, His book of directions, The Holy Bible, and yield to His indwelling Holy Spirit.

The lesson of Andrew's life is that each and every life is precious to God. Drew was a constant reminder of what we take for granted every day, our healthy bodies and minds. We learned not to minimize all of the talents God has given us to accomplish His work on earth. I looked at our children a little differently than other parents, trying not to take their giftedness for granted and demanding that they love and care for each other. All three are very loving, concerned individuals today. Andrew taught us all to be more compassionate to others.

Jesus orchestrated Drew's death in a way that took all my fears away, allowing my husband, Tim, and me to be with him here at home when he died. This event, so carefully designed by God for Drew, exhibited God's true love for me and began the healing in my broken heart. God rescued Drew from his very painful existence on December 31, 1993. It was the end of the year, the end of a life and the beginning of a new life for all of us, especially Andrew.

DAILY DOSE 9

GOD SAID WHAT?!
Luke 1:26-55

"The Holy Spirit will come upon you, and the power of the Most High will overshadow you...I am the Lord's servant, Mary answered. May it be to me as you have said."

OBSERVATIONS

Imagine the teenage Jewish girl, Mary, doing her daily chores and dreamily thinking about her beloved fiancé, Joseph, and their future together. In today's Daily Dose of Scripture, there is so much human drama taking place in the midst of one of the universe's divine visits. Let's break the passage into four concise elements:

1. God's call on Mary's life – Luke 1:26-37
2. Mary's commitment to God – verse 38
3. God's confirmation to Mary – verses 39-45
4. Mary's chorus of praise to God – verses 36-55

ANECDOTE

Like sea billows that roll in and out, in and out, in and out with the changing tide, so did my faith as we learned to adjust to the pre-natal diagnosis we had received.

Faith, fear....faith...fear...the billows of emotion rolled over us as great waves consume the shore. Knowing that faith in God's perfect plan for our lives and unborn baby's life was based on truth, we sought the Creator's strength moment by moment. Donning the life jacket of God's Word, His truth was our firm foundation.

One evening was particularly stormy for me, so Andy and I got down on our knees and leaned against our sofa to pray. In between my sobs, my heart cried out, "Oh God, we trust You with our lives. We know you are calling us to the task of bringing this baby into the world, but Lord, it hurts. It's scary, and if it is your will, Lord, please heal this baby inside of me. Make her well and fix her chromosomes and her heart defects, please. Please. Yet, Lord, we know your will may be to leave her just the way she is. Please, God, increase our faith to trust in you moment by moment. Oh, God, we want to believe you will heal her, but you may not choose to do so. Lord, we beg you to remove this cup of sorrow from us, but we want your will to be done, not ours."

The emotional sea billows continued to roll, and we continued to pray through. As Andy prayed, a still small voice reminded me of a commitment I made to the Lord years ago: "Lord, I am your servant. Take my life and use it to help others come to Christ."

In that moment of Holy Spirit intervention, my lifeline was cast. I realized that God was taking me up on my offer to be used. Like Mary's commitment to God after her initial shock of God's surprise calling in her life, I prayed, "Lord, I am your servant. May it be to be as you have said."

INTAKE NOTES

Describe what you were doing when you found out that your baby/child would have special needs:

DIAGNOSTIC QUESTIONS

What was your reaction to receiving this news?

PRESCRIPTION FOR FOLLOW-UP

Based on today's observations, complete the following chart:

Who did God use to call Mary? Luke 1:26-37	Who did God use to call you? (i.e., doctor's name....)
What was Mary's commitment to God? Verse 38	What is YOUR commitment to God?
How did God confirm His call on Mary? Verses 39-45	How is God confirming His call in your life? (Name the people in your life that bring encouragement and help to you and your family.)
What was Mary's chorus of praise? Verses 46-55	What is your testimony about God?

A Sunbeam Named Isaac

Barbara Watson

Let me introduce you to my family. We are Scott, Barbara, Nathan, Abigail and Isaac. The most sensational chapter of our special needs adventure began in March of 2001, when we began praying for the needs of a little boy over 200 miles away. This tiny fellow had been born with Down syndrome and a serious heart defect. His birth mom had an adoption plan in place, but when he was born with special needs, the adoptive couple chose not to parent him. We received a letter requesting prayer for his health and for the Lord to find him a family.

My husband Scott was the one who first felt the strong nudge that we should pursue this child. The whole idea made no sense from an earthly standpoint, but we were seriously seeking God's direction, knowing that when he calls, He provides. I searched scripture and found many verses which told of Christ's compassion, of reward for service instead of achievements, of Christ's care of the fatherless, of how he takes good care of his children, providing for their needs. This was causing a great stir in me. This would change our family forever, yet if God were leading, he would not leave us stranded but would help us and give us strength for the journey. God was working in our hearts.

Events happened quickly, and within one week, on our new son's one month birthday, we traveled to meet this one to whom we had given our hearts. We had confidence in God but oh, so many questions. Physically, his heart was not doing well, and medicines were not regulating the problems. When would he need surgery? Would he survive his NICU days? What complications along with Down syndrome would he experience? Would his disabilities be severe? How long would he have to stay in the hospital four hours from our home? How would we take care of him and our other two young children also? How would this affect our other children? What were we getting ourselves into for the rest of our lives???

One answer from God's Word that we held close is found in Proverbs 3:5-6. "Trust in the Lord with all your heart and lean not on your own understanding; in all your ways acknowledge Him, and He will make your paths straight." During this time of transition, I prayed nearly without ceasing and often sang to myself words from the familiar hymn, "Trust and obey, for there's no other way to be happy in Jesus, but to trust and obey."

Isaac miraculously survived his first open heart surgery at six weeks of age, and I survived the many days and nights when I could not hold him in my arms, only touch his arm and sing to him and pray.

A few months after coming home, Isaac was diagnosed with leukemia (AML), and we were back in the hospital for five more months. Later, he squeaked through a touch-and-go heart catheterization at age three, followed by another open heart surgery. Isaac is not simply all the medical terminology that follows his name on a chart. Our son is a living, breathing, exuberant boy, a true source of delight for us and many others. He is bursting at the seams with life-- with laughter, words, songs, ideas, smiles and giggles.

My mom calls Isaac her little sunbeam. He brings joy into the lives he touches. We are thankful to God for choosing us for this blessing. Yes, it is hard work parenting a child with health and learning needs, but the rewards are sweet. Parenting any child is a full-time job, since each individual requires different strategies and assistance. God has reminded me again and again that this parenting job is much too big for me but not for Him.

Shortly after we added Isaac to our family, I had a number of friends and acquaintances who sincerely asked, "Why did you do that?" My only answer was that we felt God calling us, and we chose to say yes to God, trusting Him to provide. Over the past few years, we have seen God's hand working in our family in so many ways, not necessarily changing Isaac, but changing us. God has gone before us many times making a way when there seemed to be no way, and He continues to teach us and direct us daily. I have experienced the presence of God in a new way as a result of God pulling us into His plan for Isaac.

In addition, we have an immediate bond which exists among families who have a member with special needs of any kind. Individual families are not alone, for other families out there are going through the same kinds of struggles and sharing with and encouraging each other.

Another benefit is that our children are now much more in tune to the special needs of others. They are learning the futility of comparing individuals, because each one learns and develops at their own pace. Our children have been especially stretched by the extra illnesses Isaac has had to deal with, because of the amount of time we have had to spend at an out of town hospital, yet they have learned compassion for others going through similar situations, and they have made new friends as a result. They are also well acquainted with many areas of medicine and rehabilitation.

One of my biggest challenges as a mom has been keeping up with the energy required to follow up on all the medical and developmental issues that have demanded attention, setting priorities which were different than they might have otherwise been. I will never again take for granted the "normal" developmental milestones that children move through, knowing how hard Isaac has worked on these and how much effort we have used to help him. It is laborious effort, but so worth it every time I see him take off running and jumping across the yard, climbing the ladder and going down the slide, or even chewing his food and swallowing it.

My husband and I were appalled when we learned, after adopting Isaac, that over 80 percent of children suspected of having Down syndrome are killed in the womb. What a tragedy! We can't imagine life without our little sunbeam. He may learn and develop differently, but he is perfect just as he is.

Lest we fall for the lies of our culture and times, let us remember the words of our Lord Jesus in Luke 9:48 when He said, "Whoever welcomes this little child in my name welcomes me; and whoever welcomes me welcomes the one who sent me. For he who is least among you all-- he is the greatest."

DAILY DOSE **10**

WHO'S MEPHIBOSHETH?
II SAMUEL 9:1-13

"There is still a son of Jonathan; he is crippled in both feet."

OBSERVATIOINS

In today's longer passage of Scripture, which I encourage you to read in its entirety, we see King David's heart of compassion for a man with special needs.

Verses 1-3 - Because of his grief, King David wanted to do something special for someone in the family of Saul and in memory of his dear friend, Jonathan, son of Saul.

Verses 3-7 - Jonathan had a handicapped son named Mephibosheth who was living with a foster family.

Verse 8 - Mephibosheth had a very low self-image. Think about the reasons:
1. He should have been, but was not, in line to be king. His grandfather was King Saul and the other men in the family lineup had all perished in battle
2. He was considered "less than perfect" in a culture that considered "handicaps" a curse due to perceived sins (his or his family heritage)
3. He and his family were at the mercy of others as they were living in someone else's home (refer to II Samuel 4:9-13).

Take note of the importance of Mephibosheth's condition because it is mentioned not only in verse 3 of today's dose of Scripture, but it is also the last thought emphasized in this chapter of God's Word. People with physical limitations are important to God. King David is a good example for others to follow. He went beyond sympathy and put compassion to action by helping meet the needs of Mephibosheth and his family.

ANECDOTE

It would be total surprise that chilly January morning. We had prepared all the details in advance without telling the boys. The car was now running, the suitcases were packed, and tickets were safely tucked in my purse.

"Wake up, boys! We have a surprise for you! Guess where we are going today?" The three young brothers shared a bedroom, dorm-style, so they each blinked the night sleep out of their eyes, looked at each other for clues, and wondered what was up. "What?" "Huh?" "What's goin' on," they asked.

"We're all going to Disney World for a week!" my husband declared.

"What!" "Are you serious?" "What about school? Someone even ventured to ask.

"Everything's taken care of I stated. It truly was.

Just a month earlier, a local church had been praying for our family as we awaited the birth of our fragile baby girl. These dear brothers and sisters in the Lord whom we had not even met wanted to do something special, something tangible, to put their compassion to action for our family. They learned we had never taken our sons to the wonderful world of Disney and decided they would bestow us with this magical gift.

We made some lifetime memories that week, in spite of looming anxiety of the future. Our burden was eased, and we were reminded like Mephibosheth had been, that our family was important to God, evidenced through the goodness of His people.

INTAKE NOTES

Name a time when someone has done something tangible to show they cared for you.

DIAGNOSTIC QUESTIONS

1. Who will be taking care of your child with special needs if he/she outlives you?

2. How do you think your child perceives himself/herself? (Mephibosheth referred to himself as a "dead-dog.")

PRESCRIPTION FOR FOLLOW UP

1. On a note card, copy the formula for **unconditional love** listed below as a reminder to keep your child's/children's emotional tank filled: (Taken from "How To Really Love Your Child by Dr. Ross Campbell – A book I highly recommend):
   1. Make plenty of **eye contact** with your child daily
   2. Make appropriate **physical contact** with your child daily
   3. Make time to give **focused attention** to your child daily
   4. Make sure you provide fair and consistent **discipline** daily

2. There are several organizations that help families set up their estates to provide for their dependents after they are gone. Here are a couple of referrals for you to peruse:

ARC of Indiana – www.thearc.org
Met DESK – www.metlife.com

"Ain't No Mountain High Enough"

Kathy Nall

Thirteen years ago, we were blessed to adopt a beautiful baby girl. Britny was born with spina bifida and hydocephalus. The doctors said she would never walk and would most likely be severely mentally retarded. We prayed that would not be true but prepared ourselves for that very distinct possibility.

One of the first obstacles we faced was Britny's eyesight. After seeing an ophthalmologist, we found out that Britny's eyes were healthy, but she was in need of glasses. At six months old she began wearing glasses. She was so cute! After receiving the glasses, she began to reach for objects! It was great to see her beginning to take an interest in the world around her.

At six years old, Britny pulled up to a small chair and took off walking. I thought of the man in the story in the book of Acts. He was sitting outside the temple begging for alms. He was healed and then went jumping and leaping through the temple and praising God. All I could do was sit and stare at Britny with my mouth hanging open. I had just been to Ladies Fellowship that morning, and we had prayed specifically for Britny to walk, and here she was walking! That was a major faith builder in our lives.

Britny has had surgery several times in her young life. She's had foot reconstruction, leg reconstruction, eye muscle surgery, spinal fusion, tumor removal, and most recently the MACE, Monti and Bladder Augmentation. Through each of these, we have seen God work. Many times, she has come home from the hospital earlier than predicted. The most difficult surgeries were the spinal fusion and the MACE. She had more pain with these surgeries. With her last surgery, from start to finish, she went ten days without food. It's so hard to see your child suffer. But in all things, God has been faithful to her and to us.

There is never a day in which Britny doesn't tell me she loves me. Many times she tells me how special I am and how she is thankful for all that I do for her. But, I know that SHE is the special one. She brings joy and sunshine to our lives in the most trying of circumstances.

As for the experts' warning that she would most likely be severely mentally retarded, she most certainly is not! She is a

71

couple of grade levels behind the "norm," but she's quickly catching up.

During her latest stay in the hospital, we had times of such fun and laughter in the midst of everything. The nurses had made a roll of bedding behind Britny and needed her to roll over it so that they could change the linens on her bed. Erika, her nurse, said, "Britny, I'm sorry, but I've got a big mountain for you to roll over." Immediately Britny started singing, "Ain't No Mountain High Enough." The nurses began singing with her, dancing around her bed. It was 1:30 in the morning, yet I laughed and laughed!

I guess you could say that "Ain't No Mountain High Enough" has been Britny's motto. After the surgery to remove the tumor on her spine when she was 11, Britny lost all ability to move her legs or bear weight. Through it all, she has stated emphatically that she WILL walk again and that she's never giving up. She is such an inspiration!

With much prayer and a special nutritional supplement, Britny's legs have slowly started moving again. She has been able to kneel, propel herself in the pool with her legs and recently crawled in the gym during physical therapy.

She's not giving up, and even though this has been a high mountain, Britny is determined to gain the topmost peaks!

HUSH NOT THE LITTLE CHILDREN
MARK 10:13-16, 9:37

"People were bringing little children to Jesus to have him touch them, but the disciples rebuked them. When Jesus saw this, he was indignant. He said to them, 'let the little children come to me, and do not hinder them, for the kingdom of God belongs to such as these. I tell you the truth; anyone who will not receive the kingdom of God like a little child will never enter it.' And he took the children in his arms, put his hands on them and blessed them."

OBSERVATIONS

Jesus had made himself available to all. However, the disciples, Jesus' own followers, thought that only adults should have a corner on the Lord's attention. I believe the disciples were suffering from that easy to diagnosis grownup syndrome – "children are to be seen and not heard" attitude. Jesus rebuked these adult believers for their haughtiness. Not much has changed today.

ANECDOTE

To anyone with an ear for music, it was evident the little girl was tone deaf and couldn't clap out a beat to save her soul. The first time I heard her sing "Lord I lift your name on high" brought tears to my eyes, not because it was so musically off, but because she had ushered me into the presence of the Lord – squeaky voice and all!

At age four, my daughter with Down syndrome was barely speaking two discernable words at a time. Every word was an effort for her to speak and for others to interpret. However, words and intonation didn't matter when I saw her lift her hands in praise to Jesus. She lowered her hands at the lyrics "You came from heaven to earth, to show the way...." At the end of each song, Sunday after Sunday, Tess would clap her pudgy hands together in applause to the Lord.

There are times when I am tempted to quiet her zeal as she sings so not to disturb other worshippers. Then I am reminded of the above Scripture where Jesus firmly tells us grownups to not hinder these little ones from coming to Him.

Once a friend was observing Tess and her unabashed true heart of praise; she stated, "Maybe those of us without that extra (21st) chromosome are the disabled ones."

"And He took the children in his arms, put his hands on them and blessed them." We are blessed, indeed!

INTAKE NOTES

1. Recall a time when you were tempted to hush a child's "joyful noise" during worship.

DIAGNOSTIC QUESTIONS

1. After today's spiritual therapy, what will your future response be to a child's praise?

2. What is your child's favorite Bible song?

PRESCRIPTION FOR FOLLOW-UP

Keep a CD of praise songs (children's or praise and worship) in the car and at home. Play them often! Make up motions and sing the songs together with your kids. You will be amazed at how good YOU feel as you and your little choir make joyful noises together!

Nina Fuller

I Love You More than Sunshine

Robin Swhier

I sit here as I watch my 13 year old son rock back and forth, the chair hitting the wall with each beat of his music. Ricky doesn't play with other kids. He doesn't ride a bike or even tie his own shoes. You see, my son has Tubercular Sclerosis. I have grown to hate that word. Ricky has had many problems due to TS, (autism, behavior, delayed learning, etc.) the most recent diagnosis is obsessive compulsive disorder, known as OCD. This one has tried our family to the brink of giving up. The repetitiveness of his questions--not once or twice but 20 to 40 times, I have to admit, has caused me to pull a few hairs from my head. I know there are other families dealing with some of the same issues every day as do I, but at times I think I am alone in this battle, in this disease.

In this world of living with a "SPECIAL CHILD" there are times I get so angry when I hear family members use that term to describe my son or when they tell me they "feel" for me. They don't know how I do it. No! They don't know how I do it, because they have never had to take him even for a few hours! God knows I could use their support.

I find myself resenting people, their lives, their freedom, and yes, even their children. I can't remember the last time I got to take a hot bath without having to hurry, because I don't know what Ricky is into. Yet, for some reason, God saw it best to give me this little boy. I haven't yet figured out why, because I am not this wonderful mother who handles each day with a calm attitude or wears the label of a super mom. I am tired and lonely at times, sad at times and angry at times.

There are times I feel the world closing in and that one more question, one more demand, one more outburst, will cause me to end up in some mental ward. At those times, I will go somewhere alone (usually the bathroom) and weep. I find myself talking to God, telling him how I feel and how tired I am. I walk out not a new or refreshed woman, but I walk out feeling an inner peace as if my load's a little lighter.

I don't know what I would do if I didn't have God in my life. It is through him I find the strength and patience to make it through another day. There are days that I find my faith tested, days I feel God has left me to do this on my own.

There are even days when I have yelled at God, screaming, "You said you wouldn't give me more than I could bear." At that moment Ricky will walk through the door with a flower (weed) he picked, half wilted from holding onto it so tight. Oh, that smile of his that melts my heart as he holds my glorious gift out to me and says "I love you more than the sunshine."

Or, he will run up to me and tell me about a train he heard or maybe he'll come sit down and lay his head on my shoulder. In these moments, I know then there is nothing I would change about my life and that I am not burdened but blessed.

I know during those times, too, that it is not Ricky who is lucky to have me. I am lucky to have Ricky. He has taught me more about the simple things in life that are so often taken for granted. Simple joys like the beauty found in giving a wilted weed as an expression of love.

Most of all, I know that there is nothing greater that God could have created than the gift of a "SPECIAL CHILD."

DAILY DOSE 12

HAVE A HEART
PSALM 37:4

"Delight yourself in the Lord and he will give you the desires of your heart."

OBSERVATIONS

Today's spiritual therapy is quite simple. We have a command and a promise:

Command: Delight yourself in the Lord

Promise: He will give you the desires of your heart (If you obey the command.)

Today's dose might be simple but it is not necessarily easy. It's actually a tough assignment but will always be worth the effort and the discipline.

We are to align ourselves with God's character, learning to enjoy Him, trusting Him instead of being afraid that we could never please Him, resting secure in His love for each of us and literally being happy, i.e., delighting in our relationship with Him. When we do this thing that is summed up in the word "delight," the result will be that we will be given the promise of receiving our heart's desires.

It is a win-win formula! When our longing is in the Lord, to please Him, to pursue Him, to fellowship with Him, our heart's desires will be what He has already put inside us. He is the molder and shaper of each of our lives, endowing us with specific DNA, talents, skills and a design for our future.

ANECDOTE

"Please, Mommy, please" Tess begged me. I want to Build a Bear." Each time we went to the mall I would put her request off as we passed by the well-marketed store. However, I had finally promised her a special reward for filling her "making good choices" marble jar, and now we were headed to the "Build a Bear" adoption agency.

It amazed me that this little girl with cognitive delays said, "Come on, Mom, I show you." She led me through the process of creating her unique teddy. First, she chose which type of teddy she wanted to adopt, complete with adoption papers. Her delight was in a soft tan chenille hide. Next, we filled the soon-to-be adorable creature with all the fluffy cotton that would give shape and substance to the chosen bear. Before we decided on a cheerleader outfit, Tess ever so carefully personally chose a satin red heart that she would place inside the forming creature. Before she laid the heart inside, she was instructed to hold the heart in her hand, close her eyes, make a wish, kiss and then lovingly place it within. "Cutie Pie" was about to be fluffed to life.

As Tess placed that little heart inside her bear, it came to my mind that maybe that's what God does with each of us. He has in mind the exact time we are to be given life, and He carefully chooses each of us inside and out. As He puts His loving hands over our heart, He longs for us to one day connect with Him. His desire is for us to desire Him. When we do, he will give us all that we will ever long for, and that's something to cheer about.

INTAKE NOTES

1. Recall your favorite teddy bear or doll. Tell me about it. Write its name and what made it so special to you.

DIAGNOSTIC QUESTIONS

1. What is it that you claim is the "desire of your heart?"

2. How long have you been waiting for God to answer this request?

3. Why do you think God *seems* to be procrastinating?

PRESCRIPTION FOR FOLLOW-UP

Take time every day for the next week and surrender the desire of your heart to the Lord. Pray specifically --i.e., "Lord, I commit _____ (name your heart's desire) to You and trust you to make it so. Help me delight in you and to watch you do great things in our lives. In Jesus' name I pray. Amen"

Brian's Purpose
Anonymous

Our son was seven months old when he was diagnosed with having a Dandy/Walker cyst. Because of the cyst, he was hydrocephalic and eventually had a shunt inserted when he was seven years old. He is a twin, and as a baby was developmentally delayed but seemed to keep up with his sister in learning the alphabet, singing songs and playing toddler games. He was delayed in his sitting, crawling and walking and even in his teething but had occupational therapy and physical therapy and got along just fine. He repeated kindergarten and first grade and continued to struggle in school. In fourth grade he was diagnosed as mildly mentally handicapped.

Over the years, Brian has had a shunt and many revisions, eye surgery and hernia surgery. He has struggled in school and has had behavioral problems. We were fortunate to get on the Medicaid Waiver list when he was young and by the time he was ready to begin high school a slot had opened for him. We struggled with whether to keep him at home with us since he was still so young, but he had been having disruptive behavior problems and our family really needed the respite! Brian also needed the structure the supported home would provide for him. Most importantly, if we did not accept this slot, it would be many years before he would be eligible again.

Brian has been learning to live with a roommate, learning to plan menus, grocery shop, write checks, do his laundry, follow a chore list - all the things he will need to do to possibly live semi-independently some day.

Currently, he is going to a very structured school where he has been successful, as opposed to a public school, where he had a lot of behavior problems and failing grades. He is now planning on taking two classes at our high school and continuing with his special classes for his senior year. He is hoping to go on to take some sort of post high school training in Culinary Arts.

Brian has been a real challenge. Now that he is becoming more independent, and soon to be 18, he wants to assert himself in the same ways his sister does. He was disappointed when he didn't get to take drivers' education and get a car like his sister. He wanted to get a job, but his job coach wasn't able to find one for him before school ended. When his sister got her job, he was happy for her, but upset he didn't have one. He doesn't think it is fair that he can't get one of the many credit cards he is offered through the mail.

Now that he is almost 18, he thinks he will be "emancipated" and be a man. As my husband and I sat in a judge's chambers this week to petition for guardianship, I also didn't think it was fair that Brian had to have this protection, but it is a fact - he does need it, and I felt sad.

When I first learned of Brian's diagnosis I was, of course, devastated that all the dreams we had for our babies would be drastically changed. I then read a book by Stanley D. Klein, Ph.D., and Kim Schive called *"You Will Dream New Dreams."* I came to realize that I could still dream for my child, that it would just be a different dream. Brian is still a person who has feelings and wants. God has a plan for everyone.

I have also spoken with my minister with a concern about Brian's ability to achieve the goal of understanding God and how that might affect Brian's place in heaven. My minister told me that it was his feeling that Brian understood God in his own way.

This summer, our family went on a church mission trip to Appalachia. In the past, my husband and I had gone with our daughter, but this year, I felt it was time that Brian went along. He was excited to get to go!. There were 30 of us altogether who met with six other church groups. Brian was assigned the job of filling our vans each morning with enough water to see us through the day. He took his job seriously. He was also assigned the job of making sure everyone took rest and water breaks during the day. In the evenings, when we had discussions about the day's work and how it affected us, Brian had a lot of interesting comments. It made me see him through different eyes. He knew he was doing work for God. I had several people come to me privately and thank me for allowing Brian to be there because he had touched their lives and hearts. Right then, I knew Brian's purpose. And, I knew that Brian would achieve his dreams, because God was indeed working through him. I know we will continue to have struggles trying to help Brian achieve those dreams, but he will be OK.

GOD'S SENSE OF HUMOR
I CORINTHIANS 1:27-29

"But God chose the foolish things of this world to shame the wise; God chose the weak things of the world to shame the strong. He chose the lowly things of this world and the despised things – and the things that are not – to nullify the things that are, so that no one may boast before him."

OBSERVATIONS

Using the literary tool of contrasts, the author Paul makes a point that strikes right to the core of our brains. Here is the list of enigmas:

The foolish things of this world are used to humble the wise.

The things we perceive as weak are powerful enough to shame the strong.

The lowly things and despised things of this world void out any cause for boasting.

God wants to shake up our thinking. In His divinely clever way, God uses illogic - the things that just don't add up in our finite minds—to brilliantly confound us and humble us. We are brought to a point of remembering exactly who is in control (He is), and any boasting we do should be in what the Lord has done for us.

ANECDOTE

"Experts" used to tell parents "I'm sorry to inform you that your child has been afflicted with a congenital defect of the 21ˢᵗ chromosome. Your child has Down syndrome, and there is nothing that can be done to cure this. Your child may never walk, talk, or control their bodily functions. I advise you to quietly institutionalize the child and tell friends and family the baby died at birth."

Those were the words of wisdom from the elite professionals in the medical world not too long ago. Oh, if they could see our babies now! People with an extra chromosome are accomplished actors like Chris Burke...swimming the English Channel like Karen Gaffney. They are delightful artists like Bernadette Resha...accomplished musicians like Sujeet Desai...and planning their own weddings like Carrie Bergeron... People who were once declared to be incompetent due to cognitive disabilities are becoming articulate advocates of those with special needs, like Mia Petersen who is a witty, lovely young woman who lives in her own apartment and independently travels the country from one engagement to another speaking as a self-advocate of those with Down syndrome.

How foolish of the so-called experts to declare the future when anyone with a soul knows that God has a detailed plan mapped out for every life He so lovingly fashions.

People like my daughter Tess may not have a high IQ (Intelligence Quotient) but they have a very high SQ (Spiritual Quotient) that cuts through the debris of this world. Their SQ allows others to be drawn into a deeper wisdom of life beyond this world. That sounds like a pretty smart thing to do!

INTAKE NOTES

1. When you received your child's diagnosis what was the doctor's prognosis?

2. How has your child confounded the expertise of the doctors?

DIAGNOSTIC QUESTIONS

1. What deeper gifts have you discovered in your child with special needs that were unexpected blessings?

PRESCRIPTION FOR FOLLOW-UP

1. This very minute, praise God for placing these gifts within your child.

2. Call someone today and take a minute to boast about something your child has done recently.

Nina Fuller

God Called Me

Linda Brown

There are times in our lives when God gives us a special calling. As a single adult, I felt like He had a special task for me. I didn't know what it was until after Jared was born.

When Jared and his older sister were toddlers, they loved to go to the playground. Jared would dart from one piece of equipment to the next, nonstop. He played hard and repeated the same routine over and over again. Rachel, who is two years older, would tire out long before Jared. She would whine to go home, while Jared continued to run wild. He always kicked, screamed and cried as I peeled him off the equipment and dragged him away from the playground.

Jared was five years old when we finally learned he had autism. While it was a relief to have his oddities explained, it was also frightening. How would it impact our family? How would God enable us to meet the special challenges which would be inevitable?

Jared had horrendous screaming fits over many things. He HAD to sit in the same seat in the car and drive past a certain house in the neighborhood each time we were out. If we had a brunch instead of a separate breakfast and lunch, his whole world would collapse. When we had birthday parties for him or for Rachel, he could NOT wait in line for his turn during a game. Instead, he would push the other kids in front of him and screech that he HAD to be the first one. His meltdowns made our family tense and wore us down emotionally. He put a damper on anything fun we tried to do.

Rachel's tolerance for Jared's constant self-absorption has had its ups and its downs. She has been a consistent advocate for him in school. On different occasions she has stuck up for him. Recently, a middle school boy was talking about how weird Jared was. Rachel responded, "There's a reason he acts that way. He has autism." The boy's eyes grew wide as he replied, "Oh, don't I feel stupid!"

Even though Jared is 12 and his little brother is six, they have a lot of common interests. Jared and Aaron both love to watch PBS shows, play with the same toys and go to museums together. They both are still learning how to share, take turns and not to tattle. Whenever Jared needs his space, he suddenly abandons Aaron without warning. This leaves Aaron confused and angry.

Jared's lack of appropriate behavior in different social situations has been the source of many heated discussions between my husband and me. It is an ongoing challenge for us to work out solutions to Jared's issues without blaming each other.

My faith in God has been impacted by Jared's life in ways I never expected. For years I had my own ideas of what a healthy child should be. When Jared didn't fit into my mold, I began questioning God. It took me awhile to understand that God's ways are not mine. Instead of looking at Jared as an inconvenience, I needed to look at raising him as God's special calling on my life.

I've never been a patient person, and yet God has stretched my patience in ways I never thought possible. Struggling to consistently follow through on the behavior plan Jared's therapist put together has been a challenge for me---especially when Jared initially reacts adversely. Even though the outcome is worth my efforts, I find myself collapsing mentally and emotionally, and feeling depleted. When I finally quiet my own heart, God always reminds me: *"My grace is sufficient for you, for My power is perfected in weakness."* (2 Corinthians 12:9) What a comfort to know that I don't have to be "mighty mom!" As soon as I admit my weaknesses God gives me His strength and grace to carry on. I suppose He'll be teaching me this for the rest of my life. It's not a surprise that my kids often catch me whispering under my breath, "Jesus, help me!"

There have been some things about Jared that have been very difficult for me to deal with. One is learning to adjust to what motivates him. He is not motivated by getting good grades in school nor by pleasing his teachers. He is only motivated by how things will benefit him. He'll complete his homework assignments ONLY to gain his free time. For example, when doing a math page, Jared will estimate the answer to a long division problem, because he doesn't want to write out all of the steps. He doesn't care that they'll all be marked wrong!

For awhile he wrote in his homework assignment book "No homework" for the subjects he didn't like. Then he started writing it in all of his subjects. I spent many hours last year leaving multiple voice mails and writing notes to his seven teachers, trying to keep up with his assignments. With the aid of some special people, we found a system that held Jared accountable. It still required follow-up on my part daily.

This is not to mention the endless behavior and bullying incidents I had to get straightened out regularly.

In coping with these stresses, I often cry out to God. I also hop on my bicycle or attack some laundry to keep my sanity. I have forced myself to seek guidance from Jared's therapists and confided in a few close friends. These things have helped me to refocus and not give up. I also try to express my appreciation to Jared's teachers in tangible ways, so that when Jared does have behavior problems in the classroom, they take the time to try and understand him.

Another difficulty I have is in dealing with other peoples' prejudices. When Jared has a screaming meltdown or panic attack in public, other people often stare at us as if we were from another planet. Occasionally, someone has the nerve to remark, "Why can't you control your kid?" Sometimes I explain. Other times I just shake my head, say, "You don't understand," and I walk away.

There have been many blessings God has given me through Jared. One of the biggest blessings is that God has opened up many doors of opportunity to connect with people one on one. In school, everyone knows Jared. I have been able to get to know teachers, other parents and their kids on a deeper level because of Jared's vulnerability. When others witness my heartaches, it helps them to be open about theirs too. This allows me to have heart-to-heart talks about matters in life that really make a difference.

It is an amazing truth to see how God really does use the weak ones to reach the wise. He can use me. He DOES use Jared. Not in the way I once envisioned, but in the way that HE sees best.

TRYING TO BE THANKFUL
I THESSALONIANS 5:16-18

"Be thankful always; pray continually; give thanks in all circumstances, for this is God's will for you in Christ Jesus."

OBSERVATIONS

Today's therapy includes three superlatives from God:
1. Be thankful ALWAYS.
2. Pray CONTINUALLY.
3. Give thanks in ALL circumstances.

"Superlatives" in context of this passage means "DO IT TO THE MAX!" No half-hearted effort; no complaining; no "lions in the street" (refer to Proverbs 22:13) excuses. This is what God's will is – just do it.

It's a lot easier said than done. Maybe today's anecdote will help.

ANECDOTE

As I waited for the elevator to open to transport me upstairs to my second period class, I was wearily leaning against the wall. It wasn't because I had been called at 5:30 that morning to substitute teach. It was only 9:00 AM and I wasn't that tired--yet. I didn't wear out 'til at least noon during this particular pregnancy.

My fatigue was more emotional than physical, and I quietly prayed as I waited. "Lord, Your Will is that I am to give thanks in all circumstances, but it's really hard for me to be thankful these days."

Right before Thanksgiving we found out that the baby I was going to have in a few months would have several medical needs and possibly not even survive. I continued to pray, "Lord, please give me something to be thankful for."

That evening, Andy and I were viewing a video someone had sent us, trying to be an encouragement. It was of a parent support group of families who had a child with Down syndrome. As each couple went around the circle, they shared that they were shocked to learn about their baby's diagnosis after birth. Some had initially rejected their baby; others lived in denial at first. Some couples fought with each other because they didn't agree on what step to take next.

I felt an answer to prayer coming on. In the very same day I had prayed it! "Lord, please give me something tangible to be thankful for." I realized the blessing we had received through learning in advance of our baby's birth that she would have problems. We were able to prepare emotionally and spiritually, unlike couples who had no time prior to baby's arrival. We had been able to research information and seek counseling for our family. We were able to pursue resources in the community for when our baby would need services such as early intervention and therapies. We had people throughout the country from Connecticut to California, praying specifically for our family. We felt God's embrace long before we held our newborn in our arms. We were ready in advance with a unified family. We had overcome hurdles these other new parents were facing after delivery.

"Thank you, Lord," I prayed with all my heart. "Thank you for allowing us to prepare in advance of Tess' birth. I am truly thankful in this circumstance."

INTAKE NOTES

1. Did you know in advance or after your child's birth that he/she would have special needs?

2. At what point did you discover something to be thankful for? What were the circumstances?

PRESCRIPTION FOR FOLLOW-UP

1. Reflect on your life **today.** What are you thankful for today?

2. On a scale of 1-10, (1 being unthankful, 10 full of thanks to-the-max), chart how thankful you are for your circumstances. (Be honest with yourself....)

1_____10

3. Lean against a wall or sit right where you are and talk to the Lord about your measure of thankfulness.

Nina Fuller

I Wonder

Adam Guth age 10

I wonder why when I was three I prayed for a sister every day.

I wonder why when I was four God sent me my baby sister, Emma.

I wonder why when I was five Emma was loved by so many people
(And still is to this day).

I wonder why when I was six Emma took her first steps.

I wonder why when I was seven Emma stopped scooting on her
bottom.

I wonder why when I was eight Emma was so funny (And still is).

I wonder why when I was nine I had so many S.M.I.L.E. friends
(Everybody in S.M.I.L.E. and still do).

And now I am ten and I'm still wondering why, but one thing I know
– my little sister loves me so.

**Note: Adam Guth is the proud big brother of little Emma who
has Down syndrome.**

POWERFUL WEAKNESS
II CORINTHIANS 12:7-10

"To keep me from becoming conceited because of these surpassing revelations, there was given me a thorn in my flesh, a messenger of Satan to torment me. Three times I pleaded with the Lord to take it away from me, but He said to me, "My grace is sufficient for you, for my power is made perfect in weakness. Therefore, I will boast all the more gladly about my weaknesses, so that Christ's power may rest on me. That is why, for Christ's sake, I delight in weakness, in insults, in hardships, in persecution, in difficulties. For when I am weak, then I am strong."

OBSERVATIONS

Paul the Apostle was a respected leader of the Roman Empire and has been placed on an even bigger pedestal of honor in christian-dom. Yet, this killer-turned-Christian does not boast in all his accomplishments. Instead, he wants to boast in his weaknesses. Why in the world would anyone intentionally become so vulnerable? We'll find our answer in today's dose of therapy in verse 9, following those two little words "so that..." Let's take a look:

Verse 7 - A thorn in the flesh (a physical handicap) was given Paul to keep him from becoming conceited. (In other words, this successful, adult man developed a special need.)

Verse 8 - He prayed for healing, but it never happened. It was not because Paul was out of God's Will. Quite the opposite.

Verse 9 - God did answer Paul's prayer, but not as he had hoped. Why? It was so Paul could learn of God's grace (It's more than a mealtime poem) and power firsthand.

That's also why God used Paul to write 14 of the 27 books of the New Testament!

ANECDOTE

No one had ever spoken to me the way my friend, Marlene, just had. "Nina, you are such a Pollyanna. No one is always as happy and "together" as you put on all the time."

I had learned many years prior to this loving rebuke that it didn't do me any good to brood or be negative. I usually covered up any hurt or ill feelings and learned as the old song says "put on a happy face." I also had this (faulty) idea that in order to be a good Christian example to others that I couldn't and shouldn't show any weaknesses. I wanted to be a "perfect model" of a life lived for Jesus, one where everything was great, "praise the Lord!"

Eventually, I began to learn that pretending I was on top of the game of life was actually a hindrance to others. No one, as Marlene had reminded me, could live up to the standards I had imposed on myself.

Many years after that honest admonition from my friend, I had to be humbled once again. We were adjusting to the idea that our soon to be born baby girl would look obviously handicapped and possess a low IQ. This was not the standard I had set for myself as a parent.

In my previous thoughts, I just knew my baby would be so adorable, so darling, so incredibly charming that she would be invited to be the flower girl in every wedding. In my unfounded, new presumptions, I was heartbroken thinking of the imperfections my child would possess in appearance and abilities. No one would ever want her in their wedding. She wouldn't wrap hearts around her charming personality, I thought.

Do you hear me once again falling off my lofty rocker? To date, Tess has been flower girl in five weddings and virtually steals the attention away from the bride! With little to no effort, she truly charms her way into hearts, young and old.

What do I know? I'm just a mom who's learning that in my weakness of wanting everything perfect God is teaching me this "dis-abled" little girl He has entrusted to me has the power of God permeating throughout her life. Now, this is something I can boast about!

INTAKE NOTES

1. Can I get a witness?

DIAGNOSTIC QUESTIONS

1. What standard of perfection have you held for yourself as a...

	Low	Average	Above Average	High
Spouse				
Parent				
Christian				

2. How has your standard of perfection changed since becoming the parent of a child with special needs?

PRESCRIPTION FOR FOLLOW-UP

If possible, go right now to your child with special needs. Give them a big hug!

Call them by name and tell this child of yours that they are a great teacher because they have taught you_____

_____ (fill in the blank) and that you love them.

BUNDLES OF BLESSINGS
Irene Costilow

"Oohhh, how cute!!! Are they *twins*??? Are they *identical*??"
We were accustomed to hearing that question while out with our
baby boys in their HUGE twin stroller.   David, our four year old
son, could predict the question before it was asked. He would say:
"YES, they're *twins*!!! AND yes, they are *identical*!!!" It always gave
us a good laugh!   These beautiful, tow-headed babies were our
bundle of blessings!

They were born six weeks prematurely with many
difficulties; the pediatrician's prognosis was bleak.   We asked
everyone we knew to please pray for our precious babies.
Miraculously they survived! We eagerly brought our babies home
and began the long, exhausting days and nights of caring for our
twins. We were so thrilled and thankful to have been blessed with
such special gifts. My childhood dream had always been to have
the beautiful, perfect "Leave it to Beaver" family. And now my
dream was being fulfilled.

Even though Kelly and Kevin were delayed in every aspect of
their development, the pediatrician comforted us with the reminder
that this was typical for premature babies. As we waited and
watched, I became concerned that something was seriously wrong.
They spoke mostly gibberish, had poor fine-motor coordination and
very little language skills. We decided to take the boys for testing.
The day arrived for the test results, but I never expected to hear the
words that the psychologist said to me. They are words to this day
that are still piercingly clear in my mind: "Mrs. Costilow, Kelly and
Kevin are **profoundly retarded.** I see no hope for them! As a very
experienced psychologist, I recommend you institutionalize them." I
couldn't believe what I was hearing! We would never do that to
these special gifts that God had given to us. I ran out of his office
crying uncontrollably.

I began to drive home, but thoughts were flying through my
mind. I knew I couldn't face the future with this diagnosis, so I
thought of just ending it all – driving into a brick wall, or just
running away from home. Somehow, I arrived back home with the
determination that I would *"fix Kelly and Kevin."* Since I had a

96

degree in elementary education, I knew I could teach them and change them – make them normal. That would be my new goal as their mom.

As the years progressed, though, nothing seemed to change. Kelly and Kevin repeated grade after grade in school, and eventually it was recommended that they be placed in a class for the Educable-Mentally Handicapped. I fought fiercely. What about my childhood dream? How was I going to have that perfect family when I had two mentally retarded children?

I was so angry at God! I was mad at the world! I was jealous of my friends' "normal" children that easily achieved and become "A students." I was making everyone in my family miserable with my unrealistic demands. Finally, I hit bottom and became depressed, lonely and afraid that my perfect family would never be a reality.

I attended church as a child so I knew about God and His Son, Jesus. I remembered all the Bible stories and the miracles that Jesus performed. I decided it might be a good idea to pray and ask God to "fix Kelly and Kevin." So, that became my obsession. I prayed and prayed and prayed. Nothing happened! Then I became angrier at God. I shook my fist at Him, accusing Him of ruining my life and my dream of a beautiful, perfect family.

One day in the midst of my anger and tears, I cried out to God for at least the thousandth time. It seemed a gentle, calming breeze entered into the room with me. In my heart, I heard God say to me: "Irene, I know your heart is breaking. My heart broke, too, when I sent My Son, Jesus to die on the cross for your sins. But I willingly gave Him up to give you the best gift that you would ever receive. The gift of eternal life in heaven with Me." This began a dialogue in my mind with God. "Oh, I know all about Jesus! I know He died on the cross and rose on the third day! ***BUT I want YOU to do something about Kelly and Kevin. That's all I care about!***" Again God gently spoke to my heart and said, "Irene, you know all that in your head, but your heart has not been changed. You don't have a relationship with ME." As I thought about these words, I realized that I *knew about God,* but I had never asked Him to be my Lord and Savior. At that very moment, I fell to my knees. I cried out and asked Him to come into my life, to change me and help me see Kelly and Kevin with *His eyes.*

After I prayed, I fully expected a miracle – that God would "fix Kelly and Kevin". I watched and waited for signs of improvement. Nothing changed! Their needs remained the same. I was in for a big surprise! Something, or should I say "someone" was changing. I noticed that I was the one changing – God was changing the twins' mother! My attitude toward Kelly and Kevin became one of patience and acceptance. When my focus shifted to accepting them as God made them, He changed my heart to unconditional love.

The Bible says: "If anyone be in Christ, he is a new creation, old things are passed away and all things become new." That is what I experienced! I was a new creation in Christ Jesus and began to see Kelly and Kevin with *new* eyes....**God's eyes.**

SPECIAL NOTE:

Today, Kelly and Kevin are 31 years old, and their big brother David is 36. They have exceeded and accomplished far more than the psychologist expected. They received their high school diplomas in special education. They attended a special course for driver's education and got their licenses when they were 19. They are faithful, hardworking, tax paying citizens. They love and enjoy life; they have taught us to accept people, to see the humor in life and to be thankful for each and every day.

God taught me that His strength is always available regardless of the trial we may face. He is our Refuge and Strong Tower. As we run to Him, He will comfort us and carry us each step of the way. (Proverbs 18:10)

I am eternally grateful for our bundles of blessings.

A CALM STORM
MATTHEW 7:24-27

"Therefore everyone who hears these words of mine and puts them into practice is like a wise man who built his house on the rock. The rain came down, the streams rose, and the winds blew and beat against that house, yet it did not fall because it had its foundation on the rock. But everyone who hears these words of mine and does not put them into practice is like a foolish man who built his house on sand. The rain came down, the streams rose and the winds blew and beat against that house and it fell with a great crash."

OBSERVATIONS

As I prepare today's daily dose of therapy, I have a confession to make. I am not home in my office, writing and juggling kids and schedules today. At this very moment, thanks to a supportive husband and generous friends, I am gaining inspiration on the shores of Grand Cayman! I am basking in the warmth of island sunshine, overlooking the beauty of emerald waters, listening to the waves lapping against the Iron Shore. All is calm today, but this small island in the British West Indies is still in recovery from Hurricane Ivan which assaulted the land, the people and their homes just over a year ago. Many of the beaches have been reduced to narrow shorelines, their sands swept back into the ocean by an act of God. The friends with whom I am staying had minimal damage to their home, even though the ocean is only 300 feet from their door.

Thanks to modern technology and early warning systems, those who heeded the signals were kept safe. Years ago, most of the homes on this island were built on solid ground, stabilized with concrete walls that were filled with cement and steel. These homes were built to withstand future storms which were sure to come. These are the homes that weathered the notorious Ivan, Cindy, Dennis, Wilma and others through the years.

These are the people that knew future storms were sure to come, and they prepared for survival in advance.

ANECDOTE

When our family was faced with our own personal hurricane called a crisis pregnancy, we were able to survive because we were shored up. Here's how we did it:

1. We started immediately to study the new course we would soon be navigating.

2. We had built our foundation on God's Word, absolute truth, which anchored us during the tumultuous winds of fear.

3. We had weathered other storms, learning the goodness of God's character in all things.

4. We had others' experiences from which to seek counsel and learn their survival skills.

5. We huddled together as a family with rations of truth, love, and prayer that strengthened us while we waited out the torrents of fear that pelted our minds.

6. We did not deny the storm was happening.

7. We were confident in our preparation. We had built our lives not on sinking sands of false securities, but on the solid rock of an unchanging God.

8. We waited out the storm and after the onslaught we gave thanks to God for being our source of strength, our redeemer, our savior.

INTAKE NOTES

1. What are some of the things you've discovered to be faulty foundations (i.e., income, job security, friends, doctors' opinions, etc.)

DIAGNOSTIC QUESTIONS

1. Are you confident in the foundation on which you have built your life?

2. I want to invite you to take a step of faith and invite God's Son, Jesus Christ, to become the anchor of your life today.

PRESCRIPTION FOR FOLLOW-UP

Knowing future storms are inevitable, what survival skills have you found to be lifesavers?

Complete the following list of personal anchors:

1. Favorite Scripture:

2. Close friends:

3. Wise advice, based on truth received:

4. God's character qualities:

Today may be a stormy day for you or possibly you are enjoying a balmy day of sunshine in your soul. In any setting, take a minute to peek outside yourself and give praise to the Master of the winds and the waves for being an ever-present help in time of need.

101

Nina Fuller

Courage Through the Cracks

Sharon P.

"It's a little man!" the doctor pronounced to my ecstatic joy. No one had to tell me how special he was.

I had been unable to conceive for over 10 years. One Wednesday night, our pastor felt compelled to pray for all the barren women of the church, and a year later here I was, the new mother of a true miracle – a blond haired, blue eyed baby boy named Michael.

A few minutes after the birth of my son, the pediatrician came in and announced there were respiratory problems and a possible carcinoma on the baby's right shoulder. Needless to say, my praise party in the recovery room was abruptly interrupted as fear crept into my thoughts and anguished questions jumped up and down in my mind.

That moment was the beginning of a new phase of life I had not bargained for. It would be a journey that would be full of tugging on the handles of prayer, releasing fear and disappointment for faith, and accepting the deep grace of God. Healing for my son occupied my desires so much that I never realized how this special child would bring unexpected healing in my own soul and in that of our family, as well.

The respiratory problems eased, and Michael's lungs grew stronger before we went home two days later. The "possible carcinoma" turned out to be a large birthmark called a hairy nieva. This time, my praise party with God went uninterrupted.

There would soon be other problems and new diagnoses – some of them correct and some misdiagnoses. Each new set of health issues caused us to look beyond our limited abilities. With every challenge that began to reveal our son was a child with special needs, new people entered our lives. We would gain true friends; appreciate the knowledge of every physician; take the advice of excellent counselors, the insight of special teachers and the encouragement of wonderful ministers. On more than one occasion incredibly gifted social workers gave us hope through dark, exhausting days and the cracks our son so often fell through.

When Michael was 20 months, we rushed him to the emergency room with a fever that escalated to 105 degrees. The diagnosis was roseola, and we were sent home with powerful antibiotics after his fever was iced down. In the weeks that followed, his responses seemed somewhat slower, his alertness a bit duller. Thinking it was temporary, I dismissed my concern and plunged into the busy life of motherhood and full-time teaching.

Behavioral problems surfaced by age four, and Michael's alertness grew worse. We had him evaluated and discovered the roseola had been, in all likelihood, a misdiagnosis. Our physician believed Michael's illness was encephalitis because the alertness problem turned out to be petit mal epileptic seizures. Throughout each day, he was having between 60 to 80 seizures lasting 15 to 20 seconds.

There was other neurological damage as well. He would have eye-hand coordination problems. We began medication, worked with his coordination and watched the courage of our young son grow. I can still remember his first EEG; with electrodes attached all over his head, he gave a thumbs-up to the technician and bravely said, "Go for it!"

Michael's courage and our faith carved out new niches in all our souls. We continued medication and prayer. When Michael was 11, his epilepsy was gone as quickly as it had come. The behavioral problems and other neurological damage remained.

In first grade, there was another development. Testing revealed our son had an auditory learning disability and he was put in special education classes. After seeing new weaknesses develop after being in the classes, we decided to try placing him back in regular classes. He compensated by developing a phenomenal memory. He surpassed expectations. I had been told he would never be able to read well. Today, reading is one of his greatest skills.

Cognitive skills became more difficult through the years; his skills were insufficient by the tenth grade to keep him on the regular scholastic track for graduation. He went into the work program of the agriculture department at high school. There were many bumps on the road along the way, including intensive tutoring in order to pass the mandatory TAS test in our state. Finally, the fifth time Michael took the test he was successful and went on to obtain his high school diploma with the rest of his graduation class. We *all* grew in patience during those years!

I wish I could say that life got easier, but that is not the truth. Michael developed deep, suicidal depression at 19 and was unable to keep even the simplest of jobs. Once again we had him tested as we sought help. Once again he fell through the cracks, because his IQ of 74 was two points too high to qualify for services to the mentally challenged. We learned our son was not "handicapped *enough.*" The frustration and disappointment in trying to find help was overwhelming at times.

Our son was dependent on us but angry and depressed with all of life. What painful years we went through in Michael's early twenties. In spite of the pain we all endured, they were the years our family benefited from the most. As Michael's parents, we needed to grow in our understanding of the extent of his disabilities and not do things for him that he needed to learn to do for himself. Michael needed to accept his true limitations. Finding the balance was an excruciating but invaluable process.

There have been anger outbursts, mild paranoia and some degree of impulse disorder. Michael's doctors have said he will need to live with us or very near us for the remainder of his life. We know that we are sharing life with a very magnificent soul whose brave spirit inspires us toward victory from our own frailties.

We have had deep caverns of truth, mercy and faith cut into our beings. Our limited and sometimes closed minds have been forged open by the keen insight of others with whom we have made inseparable bonds. Discouragement has been given a quick kick in the pants by emerging hope. And, we have discovered a love that is deeper than ever imaginable. That love pushes through closed doors, rises above impossible questions and leads far beyond dead-end roads, incorrect diagnoses, our fallible but well intentioned efforts and repeated mistakes. It is tough and soft all at the same time; it is grounded by persistent, patient truth and bound by compassionate, unearned mercy. It builds strong bridges of trust across empty divides of selfishness. Above all, it prepares us for the unknown, because the One who knows all has developed in each of us courage through the cracks.

YOU SCRATCH MY BACK; I'LL SCRATCH YOURS
I KINGS 17:1-24

"Then the woman said to Elijah, 'Now I know that you are a man of God and that the word of the Lord from your mouth is true.'"

OBSERVATIONS – *We interrupt our regularly scheduled programming to bring you this special dose of spiritual therapy.*

The key players in this dose of God's Word are:

> Leading Man: Elijah, servant of the God of Israel
> Leading Lady: Widow at Zarephath, unbeliever
> Supporting Actor: Son of the widow
> Director: God

Prelude: During a drought, Elijah heads eastward at God's command and is divinely provided food and drink until it all dries up.

Act One: The impoverished widow and her dependent son are preparing their last meal before their anticipated death due to plague and starvation. The Lord interrupts the widow's plans by assigning a task to her.

Chapter 17: verse 10 - Elijah arrives in town and approaches the widow. He calls out to her, and she sets out to get him a drink of water, just as she supposed the Lord commanded her. However, Elijah isn't finished putting his lunch order in and calls out to her. Realizing she couldn't get away that easily, the woman halts in her tracks.

Verse 12 - She declares her kitchen closed as she has no bread to share. In fact, she is making her final arrangements.

Act Two: Elijah gives the distraught widow something to live for, a reason to be alive.

Verses 13-16 - God has called her to a task and He will provide what she needs to be obedient. The widow doesn't know it at the time, but she will encounter a greater need.

Act Three: Elijah, the widow and her son have become a party of three, all living under one roof (she must have been a great cook!), well fed and well adjusted.

Scene Set Up: Picture the scenario we are about to see as a reality show in today's terms:
- Single mother and her son are living in poverty in a sub-culture with no medical care.
- Bizaar religious person whose past is tainted by living with the birds and hearing the voice of God.
- Neighbors are surely whispering among themselves at the developing improprieties of this living arrangement, especially since there was a young boy involved.

Verse 17 - The son of the widow becomes ill to the point of death. Formerly, the widow had been meeting Elijah's needs. Now, the roles reverse. The widow, under conviction of her own sins, blames Elijah. Instead of taking it personally, Elijah performs CPR (Coronary Pulmonary Resuscitation) on the boy and miraculously restores the beloved son back to life.

Epilogue: There is a cycle of care found in today's reality show which has pre-empted our regularly scheduled Anecdote:

1. Elijah, a man who believed in God had a physical need for food and an emotional need for human companionship, especially after living with only birds for an extended time.

2. The widow had a need to be taken care of physically, emotionally and spiritually.

3. The son had physical needs, the emotional need for a man in his life since his own father was dead, and a spiritual need of which he was not even aware. To add to it all, he developed a physical health need. In other words, he was fine at birth and in his earlier years but developed an illness that went undiagnosed until he stopped breathing and needed life support.

There are several lessons we can glean from all of this drama.
1. Elijah obeyed God yet still had needs.
2. God met those needs through an unbeliever.
3. God met the widow's needs through Elijah in spite of his own needs.
4. God became real to the widow as Elijah lived out his faith as a man of God
5. God's people sometimes have great needs so God can use them in great ways. In the process, we are all blessed in great ways.

INTAKE NOTES

1. Who is someone that has helped meet your needs as you obey God?

DIAGNOSTIC QUESTIONS

1. What needs do you have
   o Physically?

   o Emotionally?

   o Spiritually?

2. In spite of your own needs, what is God's calling in your life these days?

PRESCRIPTION FOR FOLLOW-UP

Look for someone this week who needs new life breathed into them. Do something special for them, but let them know it was because God placed them on your heart.

Nina Fuller

Bryson's Reward
Lisa Tuttle

This year my family attended an Easter egg hunt held at one of the larger parks in our community. We arrived half an hour before the designated start of the hunt, but already hundreds of children and parents milled about the field. I felt a twinge of disappointment as I read the age categories from the chart. Bryson would compete against six and seven year olds. At six, he resembled a four year old in size and development. Sickly since birth, he'd struggled for every physical accomplishment. Heart surgery and years of physical therapy had improved his health, but children his age dwarfed him in size.

"Good thing we came early," I told him. "You can get a spot on the front row."

He followed me to the starting line and stood smiling and eager with the other children. I left him there while I walked his siblings to their locations. I returned to find Bryson in the seventh or eighth row.

Disheartened, I knelt beside him. "What happened, buddy? How did you get way back here?"

"The other kids wanted to be up front. They were pushing and shoving, so I let them have my spot. I don't mind being in the back."

I sighed. Born with a gentle and generous spirit, Bryson never hesitated to share or give preference to other children, even if it meant sacrificing something important to him.

Knowing the crowd would overrun Bryson, I offered him a strategy. "When the gun sounds, run as fast as you can down the sideline. The other children will stop to pick up eggs. You run past them and get eggs from the other end of the field."

Bryson, obedient to a fault, nodded. "Okay, Mommy."

Minutes later, the gun exploded, and children ran in every direction, scooping up treasured eggs. I watched Bryson run for a moment then turned to search for my other children. The contest ended in less than two minutes.

With the fields swept clean of their pastel plastic orbs, children returned to their parents. My oldest son arrived first, then my daughter. We waited together for little Bryson. Other children rushed from the field designated to the six and seven year olds,

108

lugging bags that bulged to overflowing with eggs. Seeing their bounty, our expectations of Bryson's success were high.

Soon, he came into view. With a sweet, satisfied smile gracing his lips and chocolaty eyes alight with the excitement, he approached our little huddle. My gaze fell upon his bag. Only a few small lumps lined the bottom of the sack, and my heart twisted in my chest. This was Bryson's portion in life—to conduct himself politely when others were pushy, to remember to be considerate and kind when others were rude and aggressive, only to be cheated out of the reward he deserved. At that moment, life seemed unfair. He opened his bag and proudly showed us the four eggs he'd collected, a pitiful reward for such innate goodness.

As was my habit, I downplayed the fact that his performance was not as productive as the other children's. I praised him for running fast and being polite. I focused on the fun we'd had and pretended numbers didn't matter. Bryson showed no regret over his scant collection. With his trademark sweet smile, he examined his eggs, rolling them over in his hands.

As the hunt came to a close, the officials requested the contestants empty their eggs into their sacks and return the plastic shells for use again next year. We knelt down, and the children opened the eggs, exclaiming over the candy as they worked at the task.

Bryson, lacking strength in his hands and arms, was struggling to pry his eggs apart. I leaned over to assist him and opened the first egg. A slip of paper fluttered to the ground. Bryson picked it up and stared in confusion. "Paper? Why did they put paper in my egg?"

I took the slip from him and read. "You are the grand prize winner."

Emotion flooded my heart as God reminded me that winning isn't about being the fastest or the strongest. To God, winning is in the attitude.

Bryson went home with a shiny new bike.

DAILY DOSE **18**

THE TEACHER
JEREMIAH 1:5-8

"Before I formed you in the womb I knew you, before you were born I set you apart. I appointed you as a prophet to the nations. Ah, Sovereign Lord, I said, I do not know how to speak; I am only a child. But the Lord said to me, 'Do not say, I am only a child.'
You must go to everyone I send you to and say whatever I command you. Do not be afraid of them, for I am with you and will rescue you, declares the Lord."

OBSERVATIONS

God has a lot to teach us grownups about serving Him.

Verse 5 - God knew us before we were born. We have each been set apart by God to serve Him.

Verse 6 and 7 - In spite of making excuses to serve Him, God is patient with us. God gently rebukes us. God expects us to be obedient to Him.

Verse 8 - God expects us to be brave as we serve Him. God knows we will experience fear but promises to rescue us.

ANECDOTE

I had just finished introducing little Tess to the roomful of divinity students. Tess had toddled over to the front of the class, where I was a guest speaker. She waved hello to the group, completely uninhibited, and stole their hearts. She wasn't very verbal yet, but she loved music and indicated she wanted to sing her favorite song by pointing her index finger in the air, making circular motions as if waving a light. With a bright smile, she invited the distinguished group of scholars to join in singing:

> This Little Light of Mine,
> I'm gonna let it shine...let it shine, let it shine, let it shine!"

As I brought my presentation on the value of every human life to a close, I noticed one minister in the front row wiping tears from his eyes. It wasn't until sometime later that I learned what had taken place.

Long before our presentation, this man of God and his wife had already decided they would abort any pregnancy if they found out the baby had Down syndrome or other defects. Without saying an intelligible word, Tess changed all that for this man of the cloth. He shared that watching Tess's beautiful little face light up, the joy she exuded, and the love we shared as mother and daughter was the wake up call he needed. A new conviction had formed in his heart. Every life is a creation of God, and there are no accidents of life. Each life has beauty and value and purpose.

And to think, a little child who did not even know how to speak taught the class that day.

INTAKE NOTES

1. Is your child verbal? If not, how does he/she communicate?

2. What have others said that your child has taught them?

DIAGNOSTIC QUESTIONS

1. What have you learned from this child God has appointed to be a part of your life?

2. What have you learned about God because of having this child?

PRESCRIPTION FOR FOLLOW-UP

Learn the sign language to the song "Jesus Loves Me," and teach it to your family. As a family, sing and sign the song as part of your mealtime grace this week.

Long Awaited Blessing

Sondra Green

At thirty-nine years old, I had waited a long time for this pregnancy and the birth of my perfect child. My obstetrician explained that at my age, the risk of having a child with Down syndrome was fairly high. He explained that we could do an amniocentesis, and I asked him what we could do if the baby had Down syndrome. He gave me two options: abort or go on with the pregnancy. In my eyes there was only one option, and it wasn't abortion. Because of my age, a lot of ultrasounds were done, and they were showing signs of Down syndrome. Between five and six months, we went ahead and did the amniocentesis to confirm the possibility of Down syndrome.

I expected the doctor to call and set up an appointment to give my husband and me the results in person, but instead, she called and told me over the phone. I was all alone as my husband was at work. Every emotion that one could have, I had in a matter of seconds—all by myself. I was mad at God. I couldn't believe He could do this to me.

I called Scott, my husband, to come home from work. We went straight to the bookstore and bought two books and learned as much as we could about our son's diagnosis. My biggest fear was that I might not be able to love a child that is not perfect, and I couldn't expect others to love him if I couldn't. I had wanted to name my son "Ryan," which is his big brother Justin's middle name, and "Thomas" after my dad. But, what would my dad and Justin think if this less than "perfect" child had their names? Would they be proud or be insulted by my gesture.

When I thought I had myself "together" I sat down and started calling family and close friends. Some of the conversations I got through just fine. Others, I could hardly talk. Some reacted by crying, some couldn't say anything, and others apologized.

With a 15 year old always hoping to be a big brother, Justin was the one I hated most to tell that his baby brother would be born with Down syndrome. I wasn't sure how to go about it so I asked him if he knew what Down syndrome was. His reaction left me speechless. Justin's answer was "Retarded. And, my brother will not be retarded." He got up and left the room. I was further devastated.

Nina Fuller

One Sunday shortly after our diagnosis, we were at church singing the hymn "Because He Lives." As we began to sing the second verse, I lost it. "How sweet to hold your newborn baby, and feel the pride and joy he gives...." Proud? I couldn't be proud of this less than perfect child; I wasn't sure I could even love him.

Ryan was due on July 21st, but he decided to let the world know of his independence and arrived on the Fourth of July! Even when he was first born, I was unsure how I would accept him and how my family and friends would accept him.

I don't know when it happened, but God took all my fears and worries away. I love him more than anyone can imagine.

Now, to see my two sons together and the joy they both have on their faces every time they see each other is just amazing! They have a very special bond. Justin can get Ryan to laugh like no one else can.

From day one in the nursery, all of the kids at church wanted to hold Baby Ryan, and they did! I think the kids taught all the adults not to be afraid of holding a baby with Down syndrome, and that he is just another baby who needs love just like everyone else. I have asked parents not to discourage their kids' questions. I want them to learn about Ryan and Down syndrome.

One of the books that my husband and I had purchased mentioned that one of the stages we would go through would be resentment towards families with "normal" children and that we should expect to withdraw from them. That never happened.

I work with the kids at church every week, and they are the ones that got me through my worst days. The kids couldn't wait for Ryan to be born. One of my best friends' sons couldn't wait to play ball with Ryan. Little Chas, at three years old, was so eager to play with Ryan, that when Ryan was three days old Chas greeted him in the church nursery with his wind up pitch and Ryan caught the ball smack in his face! Chas is still waiting to teach Ryan every sport that involves a ball!

Ryan is close to two and is the joy of my life, always wearing a smile and ready with kisses. We are growing as a family both emotionally and spiritually and know God is at work in our lives.

In the end, we just have to realize that God does know what He is doing. It is an honor and a privilege to be chosen by God to be the parents of this very special blessing.

THE SINGER
ZEPHANIAH 3:17

"The Lord your God is with you, he is mighty to save. He will take great delight in you, he will quiet you with his love, he will rejoice over you with singing."

OBSERVATIONS

Tucked between the books of Habakkuk and Haggai (your guess at correct pronunciation is as good as mine) is another prophet by the name of Zephaniah. Let's turn to one verse today that should fill your heart with singing.

Six truths found in this one verse:

The Lord is YOUR God.
He is with you.
He is mighty to save.
He will take great delight in you.
He will quiet you with His love.
He will rejoice over you with singing.

Good news, dear reader: God loves you! He delights in you! He sings for YOU!

ANECDOTE

The house was finally quiet after my husband and three sons had left for work and school. The house was peaceful for the moment. Then, it happened. Ever so faintly, I heard my tiny little one cry out for me. And I do mean tiny and little. She was little because she was just a few weeks old and she was tiny because she was born at 2 pounds and 11 ounces. At 8 weeks of age, she was up to almost five pounds.

I went to the room and eagerly picked up my baby girl, held her close and soaked in that "new baby" smell. Oh, how I loved this petite, little miracle. These next few hours would be mine to focus solely on her. I cradled her in my arms and gently danced with her around the room. Her beautiful baby blue eyes with their epicanthal folds twinkled up at me and she smiled.

To the tune of "Are you Sleeping, Brother John" I sang my special little song improvised just for her. "Te-ess Fuller. Te-ess Fuller. I love you! I love you! Te-e-e-ess Fuller. Te-e-e-ess Fuller. I love you! I love you!"

I was delighted to be holding my baby girl. I loved this helpless little creature that was completely dependent upon me for her every need, her very existence, including caring for her special needs. Her value to me was not measured against the Down syndrome or two heart defects she was born with or the fact that she had to be delivered 10 weeks early in order to preserve my own life. She was mine, and I took delight in her. To look into her face, to hold her close to my heart and to become one with her as we snuggled into each other, was a cause for rejoicing.

That's what I imagine God does with us. Each of us is His child. He wants to save us and protect us. He delights in us even though we have caused Him suffering. When we need to be comforted, He quiets us with His love. And best of all, God the Father personally sings to each one of us. How fun is that!

INTAKE NOTES

1. What "pet song" do you sing to your child? If you don't have a song, use mine. Just substitute your child's name where Tess's name is in the melody in today's Anecdote.

DIAGNOSTIC QUESTIONS

1. What was your favorite song as a child? Do you remember? Mine was:
   "Six little ducks that I once knew--Fat ones, skinny ones, there were few. But the one little duck with the feathers on his back, he led the others with a quack, quack, quack!"

PRESCRIPTION FOR FOLLOW-UP

1. Indulge me for a moment. Go back in time and sing your favorite childhood song out loud throughout the day today. Enjoy the moments!

2. Wrap your arms around EACH of your children sometime today and sing over them. Feel the joy of the Lord as you take delight in and rejoice in the children He has given you.

Nina Fuller

The Father's Plan

Scott Watson

Isaac was diagnosed with leukemia when he was 10 months of age. At that time, I was asked by our pastor, "If you had it to do over, would you still adopt Isaac? Why?" Here is my answer: "Yes, we would absolutely still adopt Isaac."

The short answer to the "Why?" question is "because he's my son." The bottom line is Isaac had a need, and we were capable of filling that need. He needed a family, and we had one to offer him.

The longer answer has to do with how God calls certain people to certain tasks. I can't figure out WHY he calls certain people to certain tasks, I just know He does. And I know beyond a shadow of a doubt that God called us to parent this specific child.

Our story began when Barbara and I stood to our feet on a Sanctity of Life Sunday in our church auditorium 18 years ago and vowed before God to do whatever He called us to in support of the pro-life cause. At that time, I had no idea what form of action keeping our vow would take, but I knew we wouldn't break it.

Initially, keeping our vow meant participating in "Walk for Life" and "Life Chain" events, attending Right-to-Life banquets, contributing financially to crisis pregnancy centers, petitioning senators and congressmen, and voting for pro-life candidates.

Through the years as Barbara and I struggled with impaired fertility, it meant investigating adoption as a way of adding children to our family. After several years of waiting, God blessed us with our son, Nathan, whom we adopted. Then, three years later, He blessed us with our daughter, Abigail, who was also adopted into our family. Now, six years later, he has blessed us with Isaac, also through the miracle of adoption.

In Isaac's case, we received a letter from the adoption agency telling us about a baby boy who had been born with Down syndrome and a serious heart defect requiring surgical correction. The letter (which was also sent to others on the agency's mailing list) was inviting us to pray for this baby to find a loving family. Our initial reaction was, "Well, adopting this baby certainly isn't for us, but we sure will pray that the little guy finds a family soon." We set the letter aside. Ironically, the family we were praying for would end up being us. I suspect God was smiling from Heaven the whole time we were praying. We may be slow, but we eventually catch on and get with the program!

About a week and a half after getting the letter, while driving home from work on a Friday evening, I heard Dr. John Wilke's five minute radio spot on our local station. The topic was about what our attitude should be toward children with special needs – especially those needing to be adopted into a loving family. He mentioned that many were living in foster and group homes unsuccessfully awaiting adoption, simply because they were undesirable in the world's eyes and perceived as less than perfect.

After arriving home, I went back to the letter from the adoption agency, reread it and related Dr. Wilke's comments to Barbara. At that time, I told her we should consider becoming this baby's adoptive family. She was receptive to the idea, so we spent all weekend praying – asking God if this was just an emotional response to a radio program or if this was Him calling us to a task we would have never dreamed of in a million years. After much prayer, we decided that God was, in fact, calling us to at least investigate the possibility of parenting this child. I called the adoption agency first thing Monday morning to inquire about the baby, fully expecting that they might say he had already been placed with another family. But he hadn't been. The agency said they'd love for us to submit a family profile to present to the birthmother the next day. We stayed up until 2:00 a.m. updating our family profile and writing a letter to the birthmother explaining why she should choose us to parent her child.

The next evening we got a call from the agency saying the birth mom had chosen us! We were absolutely elated! We had fallen in love with this little guy we named Isaac Scott Watson before we had even seen or met him. We could never have manufactured such love on our own. Only God can do that!

What it all boils down to is this: When I look at Isaac, I don't see Down syndrome or heart defect or leukemia. I see my son whom I dearly love with all my heart. And isn't that the same way God looks at His kids? For those of us who've been adopted into God's family by placing our faith and trust in Jesus Christ, when He looks at us, He doesn't see our faults and our defects. He doesn't even look down the road to the problems we might encounter in the future as a basis for His feelings toward us. He just sees his children whom He dearly loves with all His heart.

DAILY DOSE 20

WHO YOU GONNA CALL?
PROVERB 18:10

"The name of the Lord is a strong tower; the righteous run to it and are safe."

OBSERVATIONS

Everyone knows the Lord is powerful. All-powerful, in fact. Omnipotent. Our therapy today reveals that the very *name* of the Lord is strong. Call out to His Name for refuge and safety.

ANECDOTE

The doctor had just called me at work. I was on staff at our church, directing the crisis care ministry to a congregation of about 1,200 members.

"Nina, I want you to come back in for more testing. Your ultrasound shows some suspicious elements," Dr. Ramsey stated. After the shock, I found my voice and asked, "What does all this mean?"

"It could be nothing, but we think there may be too much fluid in the baby's neck, indicating a possible chromosomal anomaly. Also, we want to take another look at the baby's heart. There is an area there we are concerned about, as well."

Going through the motions, I listened without hearing much more but was cognizant enough to set the appointment for further testing. I numbly hung up the phone and gasped for air. I immediately tried to call my husband. Busy. I tried to call him again. Busy. Again – busy! "Come on, Andy, answer, answer! I *need* to talk to you. Where are you?" Talking into the phone's dead air, I cried out "Where are you when I need you the most?"

Then it dawned on me: "Call on My Name and *run* to me" it seemed the Lord was saying. In those moments I realized I should have run first to the Lord and secondly to my husband for support. Maybe the Lord had allowed the busy signals as I called Andy so that I would hang up and call out to Him.

I should have run to the Lord first. It should have been a natural reflex to run directly to the name of the Lord in my need for assurance and hope. "Lord, I called out," as the phone rested on its base, "please help us through this impending crisis. Calm my fears and keep our baby safe." After I placed my call to the Lord, I picked up the phone and tried again to reach my husband. This time, we immediately connected, and I poured out the news to Andy. Together we ran to our strong tower and knew we would be safe no matter what news we were soon to receive.

INTAKE NOTES

1. Think of a time you received bad news. To whom did you run first with the news?

DIAGNOSTIC QUESTIONS

1. Where were you when you received the news of your child's diagnosis?

2. Were you alone? If not, who was with you?

PRESCRIPTION FOR FOLLOW-UP

1. Today's dose is easy to internalize. Memorize it and share it with your spouse or best friend sometime this evening.

2. Whatever your needs are today, take a minute right now and run to the name of the Lord in prayer and feel the safety of His presence.

Nina Fuller

Jesus for a Day

Polly Irwin

On June 29, 2004, God blessed me with spiritual eyes so that I might experience what it is like to be Jesus to someone. Thank you Lord for that special gift; I will treasure it always.

Jacob, our six year old son, was scheduled for an ABR. An ABR tests brain activity when the ears hear certain sounds. Because of Jacob's special needs (autistic spectrum disorder, cerebral palsy and moderate mental disability) this test required an anesthesiologist and operating room.

I solicited prayers for our big day. I believe this prayer coverage made God's presence very evident.

As the day's events unfolded, God revealed to me their spiritual significance. My 11hour day, consisting of four hours of driving and hours of waiting in the hospital, all expected, was really about an unexpected spiritual journey as I represented Jesus to Jacob.

Like Jesus, I was attentive to Jacob's every move and need (Joshua 1:5). There were times though, when I stood on the sidelines interceding for Jacob as others ministered to him (Romans 8:34).

There was Tom, the kind hearted man from Ireland. Jacob was fascinated with Tom's walking cane and played with it the entire time we were in the waiting room. It was very clear that Tom favored Jacob, playing games with him and asking me all about him (Proverbs 8:35). When it was time to go, Tom offered to give Jacob his cane! We saw Tom three more times that day, and each time he stopped to inquire about Jacob.

Then there was the anesthesiologist. Dr. Sonderman was an immediate hit with Jacob due to his facial hair. Dr. Sonderman bent down so Jacob could feel his mustache. It was like he knew what Jacob needed without being asked (Philippians 4:19). Jacob thanked him with a hug and then, using sign language, asked the doctor to dance. What I thought would be an awkward moment turned out to be a glorious one. Dr. Sonderman, dressed in hospital scrubs, scooped Jacob up and began dancing with him. The look on Jacob's face was what I imagine it would be if he were dancing with Jesus.

I know that kind-hearted Tom and Dr. Sonderman were placed in our path for such a time as this (Esther 4:14). I found great joy watching these servants represent Jesus to Jacob.

Dr. Sonderman arranged for me to accompany Jacob to the operating room. As I cradled Jacob in my arms, riding the gurney to the operating room with him, we made eye contact. I saw how deeply he trusted me to take him where he needed to go (Proverbs 3:5-6). I also realized how big my love for him was-bigger than ever before. There was truly no room for fear on the gurney (2 Timothy 1:7). Once in the operating room, I placed the gas mask on Jacob. He squirmed at first but completely calmed when he heard my voice (John 10:4).

I was not in the waiting room too long before I was beeped to go to recovery. Dr. Sonderman gave me a great report on Jacob, then invited me to once again climb on Jacob's gurney before he woke up. I slipped under the blanket and wrapped my arms tightly around Jacob. It was as if I was Jesus, carrying my precious child once again!

I marvel at how orchestrated my role was that day. With ease I slipped in to carry Jacob when needed and stepped aside when others represented me. What a tender time this was for me. I was Jesus to Jacob that day.

The experiences of that day emphasize the love and grace of Jesus every day of our lives. Jesus is there every day to hold us, to comfort us, to speak peace to us and intercede for us. At times, when it seems as if Jesus steps aside, remember He always places people in our lives, at just the right moment to love and guide us.

I pray that you know Jesus in this way and are able to be Jesus to someone in your life today.

DAILY DOSE 21

HANG IN THERE
GALATIANS 6:9

"Let us not become weary in doing good, for at the proper time we will reap a harvest if we do not give up."

OBSERVATIONS

Today's verse does not have a grammatical error in it. (So many misuse the words "good" and "well" but God has perfect grammar.) We are encouraged by the writer, Paul of Tarsus, to continue to do those things which we know are good, even if we are not seeing the results we hope for – yet. The day **will** come if we do not give up, throw in the towel, skip town or wave adios before the harvest comes.

ANECDOTE

My heart had been especially heavy lately. How could all my dreams for a stable, secure, happy home be so far off course? I had spent my entire adult life committed to being a good wife and mother for two reasons:

1. In order to honor God with my life.
2. In order for my children to have a better childhood than mine.

On this particular day of parenting, I felt like all I had worked towards was in vain. Not only was most of my time these days devoted to caring for the complicated needs of our developmentally delayed daughter, but one of my "normal" sons was grieving my heart. His teenage rebellion was harder to take than any diagnosis my daughter had.

I asked him, "Why do you rebel against us so much? With a shrug, his usual reply came. "I dunno."

"Have your dad and I ever compromised our walk or talk so that you don't believe what we have taught you?" "No."

"Have we ever abused you in anyway?" "No."

"Has anyone ever abused you?" (Now was as good a time as any to ask...) "No."

"Please son. Help me understand." I begged.

"Mom, it's just part of who I am," he honestly confessed. "Whenever you and dad ground me it doesn't matter. I take the punishment and still go and do what I want to do behind your back."

Some days, life just doesn't seem fair. If I had to raise one child with blatant special needs, why couldn't my other children just cooperate and be perfect kids?

My husband and I continued to do our intentional best to juggle the needs of **all** of our children, not just our daughter who had the professional labels and diagnoses.

Not long ago, I was having an enjoyable conversation with my now-grown son. I ventured to ask him why he hadn't gone off the deep end of life during his rebellious years. His answer astounded me. He didn't state that it was the great parenting we had provided or the spiritual guidance from our solid church. The biggest influence on this multi-tattooed, man-boy's heart was the love he had for his "disabled" sister. His response was, "Mom, I didn't want Tess to see me at my worst. I want her to see me as a good example and as a good brother."

Oh, the power of the powerless, as author Christopher DeVinck declares in his book by that same name. God is working something great in our lives as He uses our children to touch our hearts in powerful ways.

INTAKE NOTES

1. Where does your child with special needs fall in the birth order of your family?

2. What is the best thing about parenting these days?

DIAGNOSTIC QUESTIONS

1. Have you ever felt defeated as a parent?

2. What stage is each of your children in right now?

PRESCRIPTION FOR FOLLOW-UP

1. Make a list here of each of your children's strengths.

    Child's Name   **Strengths**

2. Intentionally spend time with each of your children this week. Tell them in specific words what you see in them that is special and how you envision them being used by God.

3. Check out the book, "The Power of the Powerless" by Christopher DeVinck. Chris writes about his experience as a sibling of a brother who lived in a vegetative state until his death in adulthood.

Go With the Current

Beverly Padgett

My husband Dave and I have been married for 23 years and have three wonderful gifts from God, all 'daughter gifts.' We also have a granddaughter, Madison, and a grandson, Nathan. They light up our world. Jessica is 21 years old, Amanda is 18 years old and Grace is 16 years old.

Amanda would become the chosen child to suffer from a series of diagnoses. I honestly knew that something was missing, emotionally, from this beautiful, sweet, tiny human being. She offered off-sided stares, suffered from 9 months of colic and had many developmental delays. She was diagnosed at 3 years of age with autistic-like tendencies and progressed through adolescence with many more disorders: Pervasive Developmental Disorder (PDD), autism, psychosis, mood disorder, communication disorder, depression and Obsessive Compulsive Disorder. She continues to struggle daily with all of these challenges. She has tried numerous medications with usually negative responses.

Once she reached puberty, Amanda became much more paranoid and anxious, making the social aspect of school life incredibly difficult to manage. She became extremely paranoid with her sisters and wanted nothing to do with them, though she was best friends with them prior to this particular stage. As her condition worsened, we had to tackle more of Amanda's challenging behavior: more aggression, more agitation, and more defiance, to name a few. Walking on eggshells remains a household technique. We are no longer able to do anything as a family. We all miss this terribly!

I home schooled Amanda for two years and then registered her to begin her freshman year at Penn High School. She had a tough time attending due to extreme paranoia and anxiety. Next, she attended Silvercrest Children's Development Center in New Albany. She remained in this residential/school setting for ten months, hoping to find workable drug therapy and hoping to learn new behavioral strategies. She struggled there, leaving with no remarkable change.

We tried Penn High School once more, with the same unfortunate outcome, which meant not attending school. I must applaud the staff at Penn High School for never minimizing her condition and assisting Amanda with her best interest in mind. She has been served in two of our local psychiatric hospitals at four different stays. Due to the fact that she becomes acclimated to drugs quickly, unfortunately, Amanda regresses.

I am her 24-7 caregiver and I must confess it is very, very stressful. Yet, I know that God has His plan etched out for all of us. Sure, it is a load of worries, concerns and stress, but we all know the importance of 'sticking together' and staying 'in love' together. We all give Amanda respect and support her with unconditional love. This concept will always prove to be positive.

The most difficult aspect for me is to see Amanda in so much turmoil, wanting to be set free. The sadness we feel for her is at times unbearable. She wants to be 'normal' and fit in, yet her condition keeps holding her back. I wish I could break this barrier. I believe through prayer, steadfast love, suitable drug therapy and acquiring the best psychologist (which we believe we have found), we can continue to help her fight for freedom.

The biggest blessing from having Amanda in my life is learning about perseverance. Through Amanda's eyes I see the longing for a best friend, the longing to have an adult relationship with a special young man, the longing to hold her own tiny baby in her arms and a desire to be a strong woman. We teach her that she 'can do it' and she teaches us that she has the power to try. Amanda has gone through so much in her 18 years of life, yet to have the perseverance to overcome life's hurdles is truly a blessing.

Life is never what we expect! Never! I would liken life to a water rafting adventure. We have to go with the current and expect to make choices, like which way to paddle ... all throughout the ride of life. Since we cannot control the current, we just have to be prepared to paddle in the right direction. God will always be our anchor.

YOU'RE IN GOOD HANDS
PSALM 31:9-15

"But I trust in you, O Lord. I say 'You are my God.'
My times are in your hands."

OBSERVATIONS

Every word in the Bible is significant. Little words such as "and, if, so that, then, therefore, but, etc.," have meaning as much as words like sanctification, justification and salvation. Today's spiritual therapy begins with an interjection, an interruption of the previous thoughts of the writer, David. David was having a bad day and doesn't deny his symptoms. He spells it out for us in the earlier verses of this psalm.

Chapter 31: Verse 9 - Distress, eyes grow weak with sorrow; soul and body grow weak with grief.

Verse 10 – David's life is consumed by anguish; for years he has been groaning; his strength fails; bones grow weak.

Verse 11 – He blames others for his feeling of alienation.

Verse 12 – He feels useless, as if he's already dead.

Verse 13 – He hears others talking and plotting against him.

David's next thought is one of those "Holy Spirit interruptions." It is the breath of life poured into hearts and minds of those who love the Lord and seek Him during distress.

Verse 14 – In spite of all the above mentioned problems, David willfully stops focusing on the symptoms (real and perceived) and acknowledges the cure for what ails him. He trusts in the Lord.

Verse 15 – He places his very life and times in God's hands and asks God to deliver him.

ANECDOTE

Robin has been one of my dearest friends for over 20 years. She is a labor and delivery nurse and has been with me during three of my children's births.

During my seventh month of pregnancy with Tess, I had developed severe complications and was in the hospital for almost a week. Upon being discharged from the hospital with doctor's orders of complete bed rest for the duration of my pregnancy, Robin knew I needed a friend's help. She arrived at my house ready to roll up her sleeves and clean so I wouldn't have to worry about all the tasks that needed to be done. With sponge in hand, Robin came in to my living room to see if I was comfortable and resting well. She took one look at me, gently excused herself and went and called my doctor. "Nina, I am going to take you back to the hospital," she came back in to tell me.

Every breath was laborious these days. I was experiencing severe panic attacks, high blood pressure and swelling that seemed to choke out my airway. Shallow breath in. Shallow breath out. Gasping for air caused more anxiety. I would try to self-talk the anxiety away. "Just relax, Nina. Breathe. Be still. Pray."

In spite of how I felt, and knowing that I had to get off the couch to go to the hospital, I thought I'd just do a little multi-tasking. "Since I'm up, I'll put this load of laundry away" I stated. "I don't think so!" Robin firmly stated. She knew what I didn't. My life was about to change.

For the second time that day, I was at the hospital and a doctor came in after running tests on me. He cleared his throat and with obvious concern informed us that my pregnancy needed to be terminated immediately to save my life. I had developed congestive heart failure, kidney failure and pulmonary edema. My body was shutting down. I was dying. This pregnancy had taken a toll on my body and I was facing eternity.

Robin, my true friend and consummate nurse, held my hand throughout the ordeal. She was "Jesus with skin on." We prayed together. I whispered, 'Lord, my times are in Your hands. I don't know if I will survive this side of heaven. I don't know if my baby will survive. Our times are in Your hands, Lord. I trust in You; You are my God."

Two and a half days later I awoke in the Intensive Care Unit. I had survived! "How is our baby?" I weakly mumbled to my husband, keeping vigil at my bedside. "She is stable and we'll bring her to you" Andy gratefully declared.

Both Baby Tess and I were survivors of the real kind. God had delivered us from the terror against our lives.

INTAKE NOTES

1. Who would you say is your closest friend?

DIAGNOSTIC QUESTIONS

1. Have you ever been close to death? Write out your experience:

2. Who did God use in your life during that time to be "Jesus with skin on?"

PRESCRIPTION FOR FOLLOW-UP

1. Call the above named person today, if possible, and reminisce about that time in your life. Talk about what God has done in your lives since then. He has spared your life for a purpose. How are you serving Him now?

2. If the person has passed away, journal here a letter to them as if you were talking to them.

Fear No More

Susan Simmons

Special Needs – a world I always feared. I was someone who would have gone out of my way to avoid a person with special needs. All the strange things these individuals did, from the sounds they made to their odd gestures, made me uncomfortable. However, I was suddenly thrust into the very world when our two and a half year old son was diagnosed with autism, developmental delay and sensory integration disorder. Little did I know at the time the multitude of blessings God had in this new world to which He had taken us.

Our journey began when Andrew was six months old. He was not achieving most developmental skills for a child his age and had no social skills. Two days before Christmas, he was evaluated by occupational, speech, developmental and physical therapists. Holidays don't go on hold, and that day, my husband and I received the news we had feared. Andrew was grossly delayed in all areas of his development and the cause was unknown.

The strongest memory I have of that day was unbelief; this couldn't be real. I remember praying, asking God why He had chosen *us* and why would *our* little boy have to struggle so hard.

During those first days, there were many emotions. Anger, denial, sadness and fear were all a part of my life. I cried, continued to question God and leaned on others when I needed strength and encouragement. In the background, I could feel God constantly nudging me, saying, "My child, I know what I am doing. Have faith."

For the time being, we concentrated on Andrew's therapies. His therapists were selfless individuals who came into our home and became part of our lives. Many shared their faith in God and became good friends.

As Andrew approached his third birthday, we began to see characteristics of autism come to the forefront. In the spring of 2003, we received the professional evaluation confirming that Andrew had autism. At that time, he entered the special school system as a preschooler. We had many apprehensions about sending our little one off to school, but God was ready to show us one example of why His plan was better than ours.

The preschool classroom we selected was chosen in part because of the teacher, Mrs. Fox. She was not afraid to approach the children on their level and challenge them to do the best they could. She did voice her concerns about having little experience with autistic preschoolers. Despite her uncertainties, she opened her heart and mind to our little boy and to our family, as well. What we discovered was that God had sent us a teacher who not only loved her job and the children she worked with, but also had a strong love for Christ. Although Andrew has moved beyond pre-school, Mrs. Fox continues to be a significant presence in our lives. It is evident God had included this special woman as part of His plan for Andrew and for my husband and me.

We have also met and made strong connections with other special needs families, especially those at church. I don't know what I would have done without the support of the other mothers of children with special needs that share my faith in God. I know I can go to any of them and talk about our circumstances, confident that I am speaking to someone who truly understands what I am feeling.

God has also blessed our church as a whole with a support group for mothers of special needs children, as well as the Special Needs Ministry that includes a Sunday School class for children with special needs. Others have been so faithful in listening to their calling to love these children, and God has blessed us through all of them. Looking back, I know God led us to our church five years ago because of His plan to care for these little ones.

Most importantly, Andrew has been blessed with an extended family, especially four compassionate and loving grandparents, who do anything they can for him. They also support each of us unequivocally in our family's journey in this world of special needs. They have listened when we cried, rejoiced with us when new milestones were achieved and encouraged us when we felt we could not continue. It is amazing that God knew years ago what we would face and gave us just the right parents in our own lives who would help us cope with our family's circumstances.

God has removed my fears and opened my eyes to the blessings of special needs individuals. He has taught me to rely on Him in moments of fear, anger, loneliness and sadness as well as giving Him praise in moments of success and joy.

DAILY DOSE 23

HYPERACTIVE CHRISTIAN
PSALM 46:1-11

"Be still and know that I am God. I will be exalted among the nations. I will be exalted in the earth."

OBSERVATIONS

Newsflash: This Scripture has all the elements of a feature story in a leading newspaper:

Jerusalem Gazette, Headline: "God Takes the Blame" by Son of Kora.

The article is complete with the five Ws and the Big H of journalism. So, grab a cup of coffee or glass of tea and take a minute to read and be still.

Who   –   God (verses 1, 11)
What   –   (is) A refuge and strength (1)
When   –   In trouble (1)
Where –   On the earth (2-9)
Why   –   So He can be exalted (10)
How   –   Through both disasters and peace He is in control

The story's take away: The Lord Almighty is with us, and therefore, we can be still and know He is God.

ANECDOTE

As I awaited the emergency C-section to help save both my life and my unborn baby, a crowd of about 30 friends gathered at the hospital to be with my husband. They were there to support him in prayer and presence. Andy was not allowed to follow me in to surgery and was now pacing and waiting, wondering if he would become a widower.

Earlier, we had to say our good-byes, I love yous, and whispered longings. Now, all my husband could do was watch through the glass wall as I was being swiftly transported to the operating room by a concerned medical team.

"Will I ever see my wife alive again?" he wondered. "Will our next touch be a warm embrace or a last farewell?" There was nothing Andy could do to help me. No more "knight in shining armor." No means to protect and care for his wife and shield her from any harm. His thoughts bounced to the future as a young widower with three sons, and possibly a newborn daughter, if she even survived. Would he have to plan two funerals?

Andy later shared with me that in the midst of all the chaos of thought, he felt the presence of God come upon him. "Andy, be still and know I am God and you are not." My husband realized that his personal earth was about to give way to the sea. There was nothing he could do to make things better. He was unable to control anything that was about to happen to the most important person in his life. This time of trouble was life-shaking, and the Lord God Almighty was a very present help in time of trouble as Andy surrendered his fears to the Lord.

With the help of the Holy Spirit, Andy was able to "be still" as God commanded in Psalm 46:10, "and *know*" – **really know in the depths of his being** – that God was God and Andy Fuller, father and husband, was not.

INTAKE NOTES

1. Are you or any of your family members hyperactive?

2. Describe their (or your) behavior:

DIAGNOSTIC QUESTIONS

1. When has it been hard for you to sit down and be still?

2. When you are upset, do you go-go-go or are you the type to retreat and pull the covers up over your head? (I must admit, I am a go-go girl.)

PRESCRIPTION FOR FOLLOW-UP

1. I'm going to venture to say today is a day your schedule is overloaded. Just a hunch.

The best thing for you to do right now is to take five minutes more and **be still.** Sit!

Don't get up to answer the phone (or your cell phone) if it rings. Don't even think about closing this book until you have practiced the art of inviting the Presence of God into the room with you right now. Try this: "Lord, I invite You to join me here and now. I want to be still in Your presence. I know You are God and I am not. Please help me remember this truth throughout this busy day. In Jesus' Name I pray. Amen."

2. Call on God throughout the day. Practice being in His presence. He is there with you.

ISHAAN's STORY

Sarmistha Bhowmick

Ishaan came into the world on a beautiful Thursday morning. The sun was shining and everything was perfect. Many relatives were all anxiously waiting outside the operating room and were overjoyed when the nurse came out with the news of Ishaan's birth. He was so little and perfect. I remember saying a little "thank you" prayer to the Lord above.

Today we are in the United States of America far away from home. Ishaan was diagnosed with autism at the age of three when we first came to the USA. Since then it has been a roller-coaster ride. We remember the neurologist of Boston's Children's Hospital saying "Ishaan has autism." That was the first time we had heard about autism. We started searching everywhere, looking for answers. But soon we discovered that there is no single solution, no miracle cure.

Autism is a mystery, each child is unique, and we have to just keep on trying different therapies in-order to help our son. At first it was very difficult even to accept the situation. I asked God, "What have we done wrong that such a terrible thing has happened to our little child? I was angry, scared and hurt. But, when you become a parent you have to put all your feelings aside and put the needs of your child first. And that is exactly what we did.

Since then it has been a very difficult but enlightening journey. Our life has changed completely. Our dreams have changed. We do not take anything for granted. Even the little things in life are so very important to us. We have learned that life is full of uncertainties and no matter how sincere you are or how much you plan there are certain things in life you cannot control. I believe that sometimes you cannot control life and you have to rely on a super power- the Lord Almighty - to help you.

Today Ishaan has grown up to be a wonderful, kind affectionate human being. He has taught me how to be kind and compassionate and appreciate every little thing no matter how insignificant it might seem to others.

Although he cannot express himself in the language of common people, he shows his love and understanding through his smiles and hugs. Life is very hard for him. Simple everyday things which a normal child learns so easily are difficult for Ishaan to learn. Brushing his teeth, getting a drink for himself, understanding the danger of going out of the house alone or running away from me in the malls are all difficult for Ishaan to understand. He is bothered by the simplest of things like the florescent lights in the malls or the different scents in the environment, but he is trying his best to cope with all these to his utmost ability. People look at him when he hums or giggles or makes strange mannerisms. Some may think he is crazy, but I know he is just trying to adjust himself to our complex environment.

I also know that he might not be smart like the rest of us, but he will never lie, cheat or hurt anyone like others do. He will always be pure at heart and closer to God. Ishaan may not achieve all the things other children do, but I would not change him one bit...he is my little angel on earth.

Life has been difficult in this foreign country where we are all alone without family or friends and without any medical insurance to cover the cost of any kind of therapy for Ishaan. We have relied on the school system and I have tried hard to do my best for my son. I am thankful that I came to the USA where the best help is available. We are thankful to God for giving us Ishaan, and I pray that the Lord Almighty gives me all the strength to help him succeed in this life.

At the same time, I worry about the children in the distant countries where there is little help for autism and hope that soon awareness will spread and help will be available for these children and their families, too. I pray that people will be more understanding and compassionate towards our children and help make this world an easier place to live.

GIDEON'S FLEECES:
PROVE IT, GOD
JUDGES 6

"But sir," Gideon replied, "If the Lord is with us, why has all this happened to us?"

You'll have to get your Bible out for the next two days' doses. We'll outline the verses here but you need to read the Word for yourself in full context.

OBSERVATIONS

Verses 1-6 – God's people are under severe oppression.

Verses 7-10 – The people turn to God in their crisis. God answers their cries with rebuke.

Verses 11-13 – God's messenger arrives on the scene.

Verse 13 – Gideon is honest and asks the very same question that you and I have asked of God in our own circumstances time and time again.

Let's see how God responds.

Verses 14-28 – God plans to use Gideon in a new area of ministry. God has confidence in Gideon.

29-35 – Gideon knows his family is not right with the Lord and has a burden for them. God uses Gideon's obedience to stir a spiritual awakening in Gideon's father, Joash.

36-40 - God understood Gideon's need and let Gideon know without a doubt that He was leading him.

ANECDOTE

Sometimes, following God's Will is easy. For instance, have you ever prayed, "Lord, we want to have a baby, but not sure if it's the right time so we leave it up to You. If you want us to have (another) baby, we know You will let it happen." Within a few weeks, you know how God is answering that prayer!

That's how we prayed for each of our first four children. We prayed; God gave. At my six-week post-natal checkup with Tess, my doctor stated as a matter of fact, "Nina, you are done having babies. After the complications with this last pregnancy, your heart will not be able to handle another." We thought that was our final answer to every couple's question, "How many children does God want us to have?"

Eight years later, God brought us a surprise! But, not like you might be thinking. The surprise of this unexpected baby was evident not by a little blue line appearing in a home pregnancy test. It came in the form of a phone call and some paperwork.

"Surely You jest, God" I seemed to think. "Could this possibly be Your plan for us – at my age? Ha!"

Having a newborn at age 47 did not make sense to us, but we wanted to be sure it was God's leading and not some midlife crisis. How could we be sure? Andy and I prayed fervently, "Lord, if adopting this baby is part of your plan for us, please make it very apparent. Open the doors that seem to be otherwise impossible. Close the doors if You desire to protect us from any selfish motives here. Lord, lead us clearly; let us hear from you," we prayed similarly to Gideon's plea for God's guidance.

Andy and I sat down and listed the logical reasons the birthparents would not choose us over other potential parents. On our extensive list, our top three reasons were:
1. We already had four children.
2. One of our children had Down syndrome.
3. We were in full time ministry and wondered if we'd be seen as "too religious."

We kept this list to ourselves and surrendered our logic to God's Will. In the meantime, the birthparents received our Home Study and called us. All four of us chatted for a couple of minutes, and then without any knowledge of our "list," birth mom made the following comment. "Your family seems like a perfect match for us. We had three criteria in selecting a family for our baby:

1. We wanted a family who had lots of kids so the baby would have siblings.
2. We wanted a family who was already comfortable with Down syndrome.
3. We wanted our baby to grow up in a family of faith.

The "fleece" we put out to God was as evident as the wringing wet fleece Gideon had asked from God. The open doors of God's Will were so evident!

INTAKE NOTES

1. Have you ever asked God to prove His Will in your life? How did He comply?

2. Once God proved His Will, did you do like so many others, and lay down another fleece and ask Him to "prove it once and for all"?

DIAGNOSTIC QUESTIONS

1. Have you ever been out of God's Will and you knew it? What was the evidence of that?

2. What has God done in your life recently to confirm His Will for you?

PRESCRIPTION FOR FOLLOW-UP

Record the evidences in your life TODAY that assure you are in the center of God's Will

Nina Fuller

The Silver Lining
Jill Rogers

It was time for Libby to move on. She was receiving services in the city where we live, from the same wonderful therapists that had served her since her therapy started three years earlier. But Libby seemed to have reached a plateau. She needed a fresh start: new scenery, new motivations and new approaches.

We searched the surrounding communities for an alternate therapy site and found one in Muncie, Indiana, about 30 minutes from our home in Anderson. In contacting our insurance at the time, they claimed that there were no pediatric therapy services on their "preferred list" within a 50 mile radius. Therefore, we could apply at the clinic we had chosen, and they would most likely approve it.

Change is hard. It was difficult to move forward, to leave the familiar, the comfortable. We hated for Libby to lose her trusted companions. Step by step we moved forward. We had Libby evaluated, with three new therapists, for the three disciplines of therapy: physical, occupational and speech. They required three separate evaluations, which was not an easy task, nor free from stress. But with the process underway, we were finally getting excited about the change! We got to the point of scheduling and our insurance company called and stated that we could NOT go to the clinic in Muncie! They had a pediatric clinic on their list after all. I was crushed! We had just put Libby through all those evaluations and had just gotten comfortable with the idea of going to the Muncie site! We had seen what was available there, and we were excited about the newfound potential for Libby's development. We did not want to start over!

We complained to our insurance company, but they seemed to be heartless. They refused to experience the emotion with us. We were forced to seek out alternative therapy at the St. Vincent Pediatric Rehabilitation Clinic in Indianapolis. It was a 50 minute drive, and I was skeptical and unsure. I secretly wished it to be an unprogressive, unsuccessful clinic so I could go back to my insurance company with legitimate complaints! But God had other plans.

We took a leap forward and landed in the middle of God's perfect plan! We visited the clinic in Indianapolis and found it to be a fabulous facility with qualified therapists, plenty of options and much promise! The silver lining was just beginning to appear.

Libby was evaluated again and scheduled for her first week of therapy. At the end of the *first week,* it was discovered that Libby had unequal leg lengths. One of her legs was three quarters of an inch shorter than the other – a tremendous strike against her balance.

By the end of the second week, Libby was fitted with new leg braces, new shoes and a corrective lift that improved her ability to walk immediately. I am sure that this detail was discovered only through God's perfect plan for Libby.

I praise God that our insurance company pushed us to go there. I am reminded even as I think about it today, that God is more than capable of directing my daughter's life. He is renowned for bringing good out of our troubling circumstances. In His Word, He says He will work all things for the good for those who believe Him. I strive to believe Him even when circumstances head in what *seems* to be the wrong direction. When dark days hover like clouds over our lives, I will remember to look for the silver lining. God IS who He says He is. He WILL do what He says He will do.

DAILY DOSE 25

GIDEON'S FORCES: 32,000 WEAK
JUDGES 7

"The Lord said to Gideon, 'You have too many men for me to deliver Midian into their hands. In order that Israel may not boast against me that her own strength has saved her, announce now to the people, "Anyone who trembles with fear may turn back and leave Mount Gilead." So twenty two thousand men left...' "

OBSERVATIONS

Gideon had been minding his own business, performing the daily grind, threshing the family's wheat at the winepress. He was actually working undercover because of the oppressive Midianites.

Astounded at God's calling on his life, Gideon tried to talk God out of it, reminding God that he was from the weakest clan in the nation. On top of that, Gideon was even the least worthy in his own family. God wanted to use Gideon anyway and built up Gideon's confidence.

You may be shocked to learn what God does next to Gideon as we take a look at today's spiritual therapy in Judges Chapter 7.

Verse 1 – Gideon starts off to fight the oppressive Midianites, just as God called him to do.

Verse 2 – Gideon has matured and has gone from being meek and weak to becoming a confident conqueror. He had developed an impressive army with 33,000 troops. However, God declares to

Gideon that there are too many soldiers and that He wants Gideon to reduce the troops. 20,000 men are given honorable discharges. (I imagine at this point Gideon gulps to see the gaps in his personal strategic plan of action.)

Verse 3 – Adjusting the numbers, 10,000 troops remain, and Gideon starts developing Plan B.

Verse 4 – God interjects His own plan and lets Gideon know there are still too many men.

Verses 5, 6 – Of the 10,000 who were brave enough to remain after the first draft, not all could cut the grade when put to the lap test. 2,700 of the troops failed as soldier-material, leaving Gideon with an elite 300 men. Looks like Gideon needed a Plan C.

Verses 7-9 – In spite of wondering what God must have been up to, Gideon continues to follow God's plan.

Verses 10-12 – God knows how Gideon is feeling (as He always does) and allows room for Gideon's fears which seem to be validated when he discovers the vastness of the enemies' numbers.

Verses 13-20 – Through other people, God affirms His leading, and Gideon takes time to worship God. Once he does, Gideon is renewed in his zeal to follow through with obedience in spite of his fears.

Verses 21-22 – God, not Gideon, brought victory to His people. Gideon was simply a person used by God, in spite of his weaknesses and his strengths.

Gideon was brought to a point in his life where God could use him in a mighty way, in spite of his family, his weaknesses and even his strengths. Gideon needed to be completely dependent upon God in order to be used by Him to do great things with his life.

ANECDOTE

After having three sons, Andy and I were thrilled to learn that we were finally going to have a baby girl! A few months into my pregnancy my dream had been shattered and plans for a perfect, healthy baby were not to be. I never felt weaker in my entire life. Just a day before, I was a confident mommy-to-be, a pro' at natural childbirth, breastfeeding, potty training. I had even home-schooled the boys.

I was not prepared for what God was now calling me to do. I didn't know how to parent a developmentally delayed child. My "Plan A" had to be scrapped, and I had to re-group under God's command. My new plan of action was not really "Plan B" but God's Plan A all along. Raising our daughter with Down syndrome has turned out to be the most spiritually defining and emotionally satisfying time of our lives. Through this new plan God has called us to, we have developed new areas of serving God and have even expanded our family to include the adoption of another baby girl with Down syndrome!

INTAKE NOTES

1. What was your Plan A (How many children did you want? Boys? Girls?)

DIAGNOSTIC QUESTIONS

1. What do you perceive to be your personal strengths?

2. Personal weaknesses?

PRESCRIPTION FOR FOLLOW-UP

1. Write about a time that you thought you were following God's Will but He interrupted your Plan A and gave you Plan B.

2. What did you learn firsthand about God during that time?

Siblings Share

Positive Confessions - Abigail Watson, age 11

When I was only six years old, I found out my mom and dad were going to adopt a baby with Down syndrome. I was overjoyed with the fact I was going to have a little brother but not overjoyed to hear he was very, very sick. He would need open heart surgery at just six weeks old and only six pounds.

When I first met Isaac, I had to wear the mask and gown required in the Intensive Care Unit. I personally thought he was the cutest little thing I ever laid eyes on.

Isaac meant a lot to me, and I remember having a lot of nightmares when he was in the hospital. My Nana and Papa kept telling me at night when I had those nightmares that my mommy and daddy would call if something went wrong, but every time the phone rang I was scared to death. When Isaac finally got home, I was so happy I said I would help feed Isaac every day. Of course I didn't do it, but I feed him once in a while.

Isaac grew and was showered with love and attention. When he had leukemia, I cried my head off because he is so special to me.

When Isaac was three years old he had a heart catheterization. Isaac scared the team so much the doctor said he wanted Isaac to come back the next week for another heart surgery.

Now, in 2006, Isaac is a very sweet, kind, compassionate, funny little five year old. We have lots of fun doing everything under the sun together – swinging, playing, dancing and banging on the piano. (Well, I don't bang, but he does.) Isaac loves basketball games. Sometimes I wonder if he is a cheerleader, player or fan because he does all three.

Isaac loves going to the library and checking out books. Not only that, he loves movies. I think it is funny when he asks for a movie. He will say, "Watch a movie, please." He can't quite say "movie," but I think it is cute the way he says it.

Isaac loves music so much I wouldn't be surprised if he became a music teacher when he grows up. Isaac loves his therapists and music teachers a whole lot, and they love him.

If anyone asks me about Isaac, I would say his sweet personality makes it hard to see anything negative in him. I think that it is hard to bring out the negative in someone when there is so

147

much positive in them. Some more positive things are: he tries hard, likes to help, is a good student, and he is a big encourager.

Isaac is a wonderful blessing sent from our Heavenly Father who cares about us. I think the Bible verse that says, "You knit me together in my mother's womb, and I will praise you for I am fearfully and wonderfully made" is very true about Isaac. He is fearfully and wonderfully made in God's image.

In Isaac's Sunday School class he memorizes Bible verses. His favorite verse is Romans 3:23, "For all have sinned and fall short of the glory of God." Isaac used to tug at my shirt and say the verse. I think it is very sweet.

Isaac sure is a blessing!

What Isaac Means to Me - *Nathan Watson, age 14*

What does Isaac mean to me? He is the greatest little brother you could ever have in the world. I like to play ball with him, and we like to wrestle. He thinks it's fun when I rough him up.

Do his disabilities bother me? Not really. I have learned that all kids with disabilities are a special gift from God and to be treasured. Isaac teaches me a lot of patience, which is good because I need more of it. He has taught me to have faith when bad things happen, knowing God is in control. God really is the Great Physician, which is a comfort to families with very sick kids. God is omniscient and omnipresent, so He sees all and He is always with us. It makes life easier knowing all these things.

If you ever stop by our area, just play ball with Isaac and you'll have a friend for life!

MISSION OF SERVANTHOOD
JOHN 13:1-17

"Jesus knew that the Father had put all things under his power, and that he had come from God, and was returning to God."

OBSERVATIONS

Verses 1, 2 – Knowing that his time was limited Jesus showed his closest friends a great act of love by doing one of the dirtiest tasks on earth.

Verse 1 – Jesus knew where he had come from and where he was headed.

Verse 2 – Jesus knew there would be obstacles and who the enemy was.

Verse 3 – Jesus was confident in his call to serve God.

Verse 4 – Jesus got busy and did what He was supposed to be doing.

Verses 5-9 – Jesus had to patiently deal with people who didn't understand his calling.

Verses 10-17 – Jesus took the time to teach those who would listen.

Jesus knew what in the world he was supposed to be doing with his life. He knew his calling was to serve God. What did that knowledge look like in everyday life? We know that God's ultimate plan for Christ was to die for our sins (John 3:16). In the meantime, what did Jesus do with his life? He let his life reflect God by His actions and words. He used every opportunity to serve and to teach.

ANECDOTE

"Mom, you've got to come home! Quick!" my son, Jake, pleaded into the phone. "Jesse and I are trying to clean her up but there's poop everywhere!"

Little Tess was in the care of two of her big brothers, ages 14 and 12. I had to run an errand and left my two oldest sons in charge of their little sister, promising to return as soon as possible. Wouldn't you know it! While I was gone little sister had a poopy diaper extraordinaire! As her adolescent brothers tried to cleanup, she scooted and bumped up against the wall! Yuck! There was, well, quite a mess in several places, but we won't go into graphic detail at this time! Let's just say I had to compensate two young men quite well after we cleaned up a little girl, the floor, the walls and some very dirty clothes.

Have you ever had "one of those" days? The kind that includes cleaning up a leaky ostomy bag or diarrhea streaks across the gym floor (don't ask about this one...) or holding a convulsing child...

You dreamed of having a baby but you never signed up for "this." You wish some days you had a time card to clock out and go home, but then you remember, "I AM home."

Whatever happened to the dreams of the past? Maybe you and your spouse planned to do big things with your lives. Maybe go into fulltime ministry. Maybe even the mission field. You were going to serve God in big ways. "There must be more to life than this," you cry out to dead air.

After having your meltdown, you gather your wits and ask the Lord to give you strength one more time.

INTAKE NOTES

1. Describe the difference between servitude and servanthood? (Hint: bondage/service)

DIAGNOSTIC QUESTIONS

1. Where were you when you had your last "meltdown"? (Mine was in a parking lot.)

2. What precipitated it?

3. Looking back on the meltdown, are you able to laugh or does it make you tense up yet?

PRESCRIPTION FOR FOLLOW-UP

Jesus loved God the Father and wanted to serve Him. He knew what his mission in life was and went about doing it.

1. Write down here, and then transfer what you write to a 3 x 5 card, your personal Mission Statement:

I, _____, believe that God has called me to serve

Him by_____

_____

_____

_____.

2. Commit your mission to God and ask Him to empower you to serve those around you out of love and not servitude.

3. Go hug one of the little rascals that caused a previous meltdown!

Nina Fuller

My Beautiful Daughter

Charlotte Postin

My daughter, Robin Carole Postin, who is now 42 years old, was born with spina bifida. From the moment she arrived, I feel God gave her to me because He knew I would take care of her.

Robin has always been an outgoing and happy person, and she touches every person's life everywhere she goes.

We have faced many health problems with Robin, but my husband and I learned early to take one thing at a time. There were even days when it was one second at a time, but Robin has brought so much joy to our lives. It has all been so worthwhile.

Robin is in a wheelchair and has no control over her bowels or bladder. Even so, we have always taken her everywhere we go. Robin has been to Canada, Florida, Washington, D.C., and even the Rocky Mountains. She loves movies and country music, as well as gospel music. She loves to bowl, so I started a league for handicapped people in our hometown. Robin is a pretty good bowler. In fact, there are quite a few times she even beats me!

As for some of her medical problems, she has had everything from her tonsils removed to having her head opened to stop spinal fluid from draining through her nose. Not counting all of the times she has been in the hospital for kidney infections and other problems, she has had 10 surgeries. The last was in 2002 to have a stoma put in to assist with bladder function.

I once had someone ask if I had known in advance what the problems with Robin were going to be would I have aborted her. I can tell you the answer is a big loud "no," because I could not love a child anymore than I do Robin.

All I can say is God bless all of you. Thank you for letting me tell you about my beautiful daughter.

LABOR IN VAIN
ISAIAH 49:3-4

"The Lord said to me, 'You are my servant in whom I will display my splendor.' But I said, 'I have labored to no purpose; I have spent my strength in vain and for nothing. Yet what is due me is in the Lord's hand, and my reward is with my God.' "

OBSERVATIONS

Verse 3 – The Lord wants to use you as a vessel in which to display his greatness.

Verse 4 – In spite of the fact that we often feel spent and used up, we must remember that God will reward us as we submit to Him.

ANECDOTE

Imagine going through labor and delivery only to bring forth a stillborn baby or a baby with major birth defects. Nine months of tender care of your body to protect the little life growing inside you. Forty weeks (give or take a few) of abstaining from caffeine, nicotine, alcohol, sodium and carnival rides. Almost a year of dreaming of a beautiful new baby to love, show off and pour your heart into. Then come the hee-hee-whos (you know, the breathing techniques that are *supposed* to help relax you) for hours on end, not to mention the excruciating pain of labor. Never on earth has there been such intensity. There is no greater pain than this and no greater profound joy than the minute you have pushed new life into this world. You cry with a mixture of joy and relief when you hear that healthy, piercing wail of your baby's first cry.

What happens, however, if you go through the trauma of pregnancy, labor and delivery in vain? Your baby enters without a sound. Her heartbeat is faint, if any at all. Your time with this child is brief and heart-wrenching. Was your effort in vain? Was your expended strength wasted?

Maybe your child actually survives birth but everything goes wrong and your delivery results in producing a baby that is born with severe birth defects and your lives are changed in an instant. Your entire family has been altered, and you are now the mother of a handicapped child, possibly vegetative and seemingly powerless.

INTAKE NOTES

1. Have you ever felt your labor was in vain?

2. Maybe you have not had to physically labor to get your children. How did you become a parent: ___vaginal delivery ___C-section ___adoption

3. What type of labor(s) did you have to go through to get your children?

DIAGNOSTIC QUESTIONS

1. God intentionally and purposefully gave each of your children to you, including your child with special needs. What contribution does each of your children make to this world so far?

PRESCRIPTION FOR FOLLOW UP

1. I'd like to suggest you get a new notebook or separate journal today and begin to take time to record the birth stories of each of your children. You might even have both biological children and adopted children! How wonderful that is! Record the stories of how each of your children came into your lives. In the years to come, they will love hearing how much effort went into caring for them before they have their own memories of your love.

2. If you have lost a child through miscarriage, stillbirth or sometime after birth, try to work through their story and write about their short-lived life. It was valuable, no matter the length of days this precious loved one lived. Write here their name and what you think the purpose of their life was.

3. Take comfort today in knowing that your reward from the Lord will surely come!

Nina Fuller

Letting Go of Kaylin

Becky Mischler

In March of 1991, I was due with our second child, this time-- a girl! My husband, Joe, and I were so thrilled. Joe and Brian could do all the father and son things such as hunting, fishing and playing ball. Our daughter and I would enjoy doing all the mother-daughter things like shopping, going to lunch, slumber parties and makeovers. Friends from work had given me a baby shower, the nursery was ready and we were awaiting the exciting day baby Kaylin would arrive.

Five days before my due date, I had not felt any movement. Joe and I were praying everything would be fine, but deep down I knew something was drastically wrong. We called my doctor, and he met us at the hospital. I asked God for the strength to deal with whatever lay ahead. Kaylin Brianne was delivered by cesarean section late morning, stillborn. She was seven pounds, two ounces, with a full head of dark hair, dainty features and 10 sweet little fingers and toes.

She looked so perfect and serenely beautiful as I held her. It was so strange that she wasn't moving after all those months of being so active within my stomach, doing flips and kicking me in the ribs. Letting go of Kaylin was the most difficult and painful feeling I'd ever experienced. I had to keep telling myself that she was, and is, in a much more wonderful place than here, and someday we will be with her again in Heaven.

All my dreams for my little girl were taken away from me that day. I kept asking the Lord, "Why? Why, Kaylin?" There were so many feelings to deal with: shock, denial, anger, depression, as well as the postpartum depression.

Joe and my parents were right there with me, encouraging me to be strong, not to lose my faith and not to doubt God. He has a plan for everything in life. I finally felt at peace when I accepted the fact that Kaylin was fortunate to go straight to the Kingdom of Heaven and be with the Lord our God. She is our little angel in Heaven.

WE'RE IN THIS TOGETHER
ECCLESIATES 4:9-12

"Two are better than one because they have a good return for their work. If one falls down his friend can help him up, but pity the man who falls and has no one to help him up. Also, if two lie down together, they will keep warm. But how can one keep warm alone? Tho' one may be overpowered, two can defend themselves. A cord of three strands is not quickly broken."

OBSERVATIONS

Why are two better than one? Here's why:

Verse 9 – Two have a good return for their work.

Here's how:

Verse 10 – If one falls down, his friend can help him up (pity upon the lonely man).

Here's another reason why two are better than just one:

Verse 11 – If two lie down together, they will keep warm.

Not done yet! Here's another reason to support the fact that no man is an island:

Verse 12 – Though one may be overpowered, two can defend themselves.

If that's not enough support that one is the loneliest number, here's more proof:

Verse 12 – There's strength in numbers as evidenced in the fact that a cord of THREE strands is not quickly broken.

ANECDOTE

We were on our way to visit a family who recently had a baby born with Down syndrome. Before we hopped in the car, I grabbed the scrapbook I had enjoyed putting together and titled "Living Proof of Tess's Quality of Life."

That first year of our baby's life was full of "firsts" and not just for her. Baby books are full of firsts – first word, first tooth, first steps, so on. There are no pages for "first diagnosis," "first open heart surgery," "first ambulance ride" or "first seizure."

However, our first year with a baby with multiple health needs was better than we had ever anticipated. We had captured some great photos of our new baby and our family that conveyed a very normal, happy life for all of us.

When we were new to the world of parenting a baby with special needs we felt pretty isolated. We gradually learned the ropes of this strange, new world and became concerned for other parents yet to enter the journey.

Every so often one of our local hospitals would call me to come meet a new family who had just delivered a baby with Down syndrome.

As we arrived at the home of another new family, we introduced ourselves and darling, little Tess. I pulled out my scrapbook and began to turn the pages, showing our new friends the quality of life our daughter, and truly, our entire family enjoyed. We saw a glimmer of hope in their anxious eyes. "We want you to know that having a child with Down syndrome is a different journey, but it will be a very fulfilling and rewarding adventure. Hold your baby and love her like you do your other children. She is your baby first and foremost. Her diagnosis is secondary. Love her! Love her! Love her!"

Similar introductions have followed through the years and our tri-somy 21 community now has a parent network that offers **S**upport...**M**anagement...**I**nformation...**L**ove...and ...**E**ncouragement **(S.M.I.L.E. on Down Syndrome)** to thousands of people in our tri-state area.

Many of our closest friendships are with other families who are raising children with the same diagnosis. We understand each other. We rejoice with each child's latest milestones, whereas other parents may take their children's development for granted. Where else besides a parent support network will a dad get applause when he stands in a group of people and declares, "This week our five year old poopied in the potty for the first time!" Or, a mom stands and through tears states, "Her doctor told us she'd never speak, yet today I clearly heard Erin say, 'I wuv oo, mamma."

Being in a group of friends in need together, we can network information, ideas, questions, sorrows, joys, prayers and encouragement with compassion and empathy. It's the friends who've been where we are, and it's people who are coming up behind us that create the three-stranded cord in our lives. The strength that we build in this braided fashion cannot be quickly broken.

INTAKE NOTES

1. Are you involved with a support group?

2. If not, could you start one?

DIAGNOSTIC QUESTIONS

1. How do you feel about your network of friendships?

2. Do you feel isolated or supported as you parent?

PRESCRIPTION FOR FOLLOW-UP

1. If you are in a support group (i.e., parent network) call the leader or write a note to them today. Thank them for their efforts. They carry the extra responsibilities not only of their child, but the needs of each family in your support group.

2. Pray for those in positions of leadership both at your church and in the community. Ask God to give these leaders the wisdom, compassion and energy they need.

Nina Fuller

Our Treasure - A Story for Jeff

By Hillary Key

Once upon a time a young man, full of the dreams of every good man met a young woman full of the same. In their search for treasure they found each other while walking the same narrow path. They knew their fortune, for many never receive such a gift. Their love was warmth in cold and sunlight in rain. Cold did come and so did rain. But they continued down the path together valuing the gift all the more.

Soon they longed to take this treasure and invest it in a dream they shared before they met. Although many around them had realized this very dream, they did not take something so precious for granted. The cold and rain had humbled their hearts.

They were full of grateful anticipation as they journeyed down the path towards their dream. They knew this treasure would shine so bright it would offset the cold and rain. They prepared so carefully for the day of truth that they sometimes became distracted along the path.

Finally the day arrived for them to realize their dream and receive their gift. Their hearts ran over with nervous and joyful expectation.

They could see their gift in the distance wrapped in a bow. They ran to it and began to open it with careful happy tears.

"Here it is!" exclaimed the young man to his happy weary wife, as she peered inside at this precious gift whose shine was not so bright. Something was wrong. They both broke inside... Its luster was not the same as the treasures others had so easily acquired. This was not the gift their hearts had seen, but it was the one they loved.

They knew that for the rest of their journey they would walk with joy and with sorrow. They mourned the loss of the dream of the bright shining treasure and envied the many who possessed it.

At the same time, they were thankful for the privilege of being entrusted with the gift at all. To lose it would leave them with an emptiness no treasure could replace.

They cursed the thought of more rain and cold but remembered the One who took them down the narrow path and led them to one another... the One who gave them this precious gift whose luster was different than any other.

As they looked through the eyes of the Giver, the One whose love is warmth in cold and sunlight in rain, they could see their treasure's shine, a reflection of the Pathmaker's love, whose luster is different than any other.

Though sorrow is an unwanted guest who frequents their walk down the path, hope and love are their companions. Love adores the treasure and Hope knows there is no limit to how bright it may shine.

Once upon a time, a young man full of the dreams of every good man met a young woman full of the same. They learned that dreams belong to the One from whom all good gifts come. And loving the gift you are given for however long you're honored to possess it is the real treasure.

DAILY DOSE 29

GOOD FOR THE SOUL
ROMANS 10:8-11

"If you confess with your mouth 'Jesus is Lord' and believe in your heart that God raised him from the dead, you will be saved."

OBSERVATIONS

Verse 8 – The word is near you – so near, it is in you in two places:
    1. Your mouth
    2. Your heart

You've been reading God's Word every day throughout this spiritual therapy. You should be experiencing renewed strength and stamina. Can you feel it? With today's dose of therapy, I want to encourage you to claim the truths presented in this passage.

    1. If you confess with your mouth (say it out loud) – Jesus is Lord, and
    2. If you believe in your heart (have faith) God raised Him from the dead,
(You can be assured of this)
    3. You WILL be saved!

ANECDOTE

"This is one crazy character," I whispered to my friend, Gina, referring to the star of the show as we slid into our seats at the stadium. My five year old, Tess, was scooting into her seat between us and she was ready to sing along with Psalty, the singing songbook. Psalty was in town, performing and entertaining hundreds of children with a special message of Jesus's love.

I would soon be slipping out of my seat to help counsel the children who would be responding to Psalty's invitation to pray and ask Jesus into their hearts. The program was lively and colorful; each character was animated and charismatic as they encouraged interaction from all of us.

"If you're happy and you know it, clap your hands."

"Father Abraham had many sons..."

"Jesus Loves Me this I know..."

Tess thoroughly loved the songs and tried to sing along, even though her verbal skills were limited. She was just as animated as the characters and she was drawn into the stories and lessons Psalty shared.

As the program wound down, I nodded to Gina that it was time for me to take my place down front. I wanted to be in place and ready to help lead a group of little ones to Jesus. I would share Bible verses with them and pray with them.

Psalty gently said to everyone, "And now, boys and girls, I want you to close your eyes and bow your head. We're going to talk to Jesus. If you understand that Jesus wants to be your friend and live in your heart, you can say this prayer with me right now: Dear Jesus, Thank you for your love." Psalty paused and children prayed. He continued, "I believe You died on the cross for me. Come into my heart today. I love you, Jesus. Amen."

It was a great feeling for me to be in the midst of this group of little ones and to be able to pray with them. As I returned to my seat, Gina had tears in her eyes. "Guess what happened while you were gone," Gina said. "Tess bowed her head, folded her hands and said **every** word of the prayer. She just asked Jesus into her heart!" She understood! My little girl with the verbal skills of someone half her age was able to confess with her mouth and believe in her heart that Jesus was Lord!

INTAKE NOTES

1. Do you remember a time in your life that you have confessed and believed in Jesus?

2. When is your spiritual birthday?

DIAGNOSTIC QUESTIONS

1. If you do not remember your spiritual birth, I encourage you to make today your spiritual birthday by inviting Jesus Christ into your life by doing just as Tess did.

2. Write down today's date and record it here as a certificate of spiritual birth.

PRESCRIPTION FOR FOLLOW-UP

1. Pray with your children today. Make it a habit in your family to pray together.

2. If your child is non-verbal, do not assume they are non-receptive to spiritual truths. You'd be amazed at how much these little ones instinctively understand Jesus' love.

3. The Word is near you. Read your Bible daily and you'll grow, grow, grow!

No Coincidence

Cindy Huston

I was one of those moms who said I would never have prenatal testing. But after suffering a miscarriage, I decided that I could use all the information I could get. About 20 weeks into my pregnancy, the results came back and indicated there was a good chance that this baby could have Down syndrome. Putting it in God's hands, my husband and I made the choice not to have an amniocentesis and risk another miscarriage. I put the thought out of my head, but the seed was already planted.

In the meantime, we had been visiting different churches and praying for the Lord's guidance in finding a church home for our family. With just a month to go in my pregnancy, we walked into a new church and sat down in a pew that just happened to have a woman with her five year old son who had Down syndrome. Then I picked up the bulletin. Chris Burke, the famous actor with Down syndrome, was speaking at this church the very same evening. He was in town for the annual Buddy Walk. My heart skipped a beat. Was it a coincidence – or was God trying to prepare us for what was coming?

Just over a month later, I found the answer to my question. After the doctor gave us the news, I wish I could say my first feelings were happy ones. But in all honestly, I was very sad and scared. I spent that first day wondering what the future held for this little one and for our family. But at 9:00 that night, a nurse appeared in my room with the name of a lady who had a child with Down syndrome and had begun a support group for parents. Knowing I probably wouldn't make the call on my own, she dialed the number and handed me the phone. That phone call gave me the hope I needed. I wasn't alone. There were other parents raising children with Down syndrome, and they were doing okay. In fact, they were doing GREAT. But that's not all I found out. The lady I spoke with offered to pray with me. Then she asked if we had a church home and invited us to her church. You guessed it – it was the same lady I sat next to at church just a few weeks earlier. It confirmed what I'd known all along – there are no coincidences – only God speaking to us, if we are only willing to listen.

Not only did we find a church home, but we found some wonderful friends who introduced us to the world of Down syndrome. I found out that it's a better world than I would have ever predicted. Prior to his birth, we chose the name Matthew because it means "gift from God." Little did we know what a wonderful gift he would be. It has been a physical, emotional and, as you can see, a spiritual journey. Matthew has filled our hearts beyond capacity. He has taught me the true meaning of unconditional love. He has given me the ability to reach out to others with different abilities. And he has shown me the purest form of joy in his carefree spirit. I simply can't imagine life without him.

SHALLOW SAL
PHILIPPIANS 3:10-14

"I want to know Christ and the power of his resurrection and the fellowship of sharing in his sufferings."

OBSERVATIONS

Let's break this verse into parts so you can see the whole:

Verse 10: I want to know:

    1. Christ
       And
    2. The power of his resurrection
       And
    3. The fellowship of sharing in his sufferings

It is the final third that we will concentrate on during today's spiritual therapy.

ANECDOTE

Shallow people. We all know a few. We work with a few. We even go to church with a few. They are nice enough people, but there's no substance to them. They seem to talk in clichés and never seem to "get it" when you begin to open up and admit you're having a rough day.

You're at the grocery store and a casual friend, Sally, sees you. "How are you, dear?" Sal asks as she's glancing at the latest in-print gossip. "Well, honestly," you begin, "I've been up all night with my youngest. Her apnea monitor kept going off, and we had very little sleep last night or the night before."

"Oh, honey," Sal snaps her gum and replies, "I know whatcha mean. I am so tired today. Last night I watched the entire DVD collection of Friends, and I can hardly think today."

You are too kind to say out loud, but you think to yourself, *"What was your excuse yesterday, lady?"* Instead, you faintly smile and are glad that you are next in line at the checkout. You wave bye to Shallow Sal and can't wait until Sunday's parent network meeting where you'll be among like-minded friends.

There is a certain distinct fellowship of those who suffer together. There's a kinship of hearts, minds, emotions and souls when you endure hardship with others that the rest of those around you can't comprehend. It's not really their fault, but you wouldn't consider them soul mates or close friends.

As each of us continues to raise our families and meet the intense needs of our differently-abled dependents, we understand suffering on many levels. We "get it" when someone in the support group shares that they struggle with the myriads of appointments, therapists, new medicines, new doctors, secondary diagnoses, another hospital stay, insurance claims, too little time, too much income (for assistance), too many demands and the daunting list goes on.

We don't wish it on anyone, but it's nice to have friends who understand our suffering.

Maybe that's how Jesus feels. Maybe we should line up our litany of sufferings against His and see if we can even come close to understanding what the Son of God endured for each of us.

INTAKE NOTES

1. Have you been guilty of resentment towards the Shallow Sals in your life?

DIAGNOSTIC QUESTIONS

1. Off the top of your head, complete the following list:

Things I've Suffered:

Things Jesus Suffered:

2. In what ways can you relate to Jesus' sufferings through your own experiences?

PRESCRIPTION FOR FOLLOW-UP

Go to Jesus right now and fellowship with Him. Don't get distracted by the things around you – not even any tempting in-print gossip. Pour your heart out to Him as if He were on the other end of the line. He is a friend who truly wants to know how you are feeling and is ready to listen and share the events of your life.

Nina Fuller

Overnight Miracle

Donna Dujmovich

Our son, Evan, who is now 28 months old, was born with torticollis. It was not officially diagnosed until he was six months old. At seven months, Evan started physical therapy in our home. By the second session his therapist discovered he had very low muscle tone and started working on that issue as well as the torticollis. After several months of therapy we noticed Evan was just not reaching normal developmental milestones. In addition, there were other physical alarms: tremors on the left side of his body, one eye turning in, off the chart head size and regression of things he once was doing. We knew something was terribly wrong.

His therapist urged us to see a neurologist, so we made an appointment with one at Children's Memorial Hospital. Evan was 21 months old when an MRI revealed he had a brain tumor. The neurologist and neurosurgeon both agreed that his tumor appeared to be malignant. The crushing news whirled around in our heads. 50/50 survival rates, chemotherapy, emergency surgery, hydrocephalus. I felt numb; it was as if they were giving us a death sentence. Through all the fears and immense grief, God ministered to me telling me, "I know exactly how you feel, remember I gave my only Son." God have me peace that surpassed all understanding and comfort through all my sobbing tears. My husband started making phone calls that night asking for prayer support as Evan faced surgery scheduled for the next day.

Many family and friends stood by our side the entire day offering us love and support. Evan's surgery took over seven hours. When the surgery was completed, the neurosurgeon came out to tell us the most exciting news. "The tumor appeared to be benign." We were all rejoicing and praising the Lord.

Several days later the pathology report confirmed the tumor was indeed benign. Evan had a juvenile polycystic astrocytoma on his cerebellum. We know that it was God who heard the cries of his people and performed a miracle overnight, changing Evan's tumor from malignant to benign.

Every day I am in awe that God showed us such great mercy. We do nothing to deserve his goodness. It is all because of who He is.

Evan and I had a long three weeks in the hospital, and he had a long journey of recovery once we got home. This whole experience and his developmental delays have indeed affected our entire family. He continued physical therapy, occupational therapy and speech therapy. Life in our home was overwhelmingly. We were busy with therapy four times a week as well as working with him every day; home schooling his big sisters; and working around Dad's shift work. There were days when I wanted to hide in my closet, but God reminded me, "My grace is sufficient for you, for My strength is made perfect in weakness. Therefore most gladly I will rather boast in my infirmities, that the power of Christ may rest upon me. Therefore I take pleasure in infirmities, in reproaches, in needs, in persecutions, in distresses, for Christ's sake. For when I am weak, then I am strong." 2 Corinthians 12:9-10.

I have always thought to myself, "I want my faith to be stretched, but I don't want God to use my children to stretch me." Well, God had a different plan when He chose to use Evan. God knows exactly what we need. I can see so clearly now, several months later, how God has used this situation for the good in so many ways. Our family has realized that through the dark days God teaches us the most. Evan's big sisters, Leah age 12, and Olivia age nine, have learned to be more flexible, understanding, compassionate and dependent on God. My husband and I learned the same in addition to prioritizing and trying not to sweat the small stuff (those things that have no eternal value).

Evan brings such joy to us all. We know God must have a wonderful plan for Evan. It reminds me of Jeremiah 29:11--For I know the thoughts that I think toward you, says the Lord, thoughts of peace and not of evil, to give you a future and a hope. Our biggest prayer now is that Evan receives Christ as his personal savior.

We live with daily challenges because of Evan's tumor. Because it was on his cerebellum, which controls balance and coordination, he still has not fully regained that function. That, in addition to his low muscle tone and being big for his age, makes walking quite a struggle. Evan also has to go back to Children's Memorial every three months for an MRI to make sure his tumor is not growing back or that the hydrocephalus has not returned.

I have such compassion for parents who deal with any type of handicap with their children. I believe God gives special grace for those parents who have children with any kind of physical infirmity. We only have to believe in Him and ask for His strength.

DAILY DOSE 31

CONJOINED HEARTS
JOHN 15:13

"Greater love has no one than this, that he lay down his life for his friends...this is my command to love each other."

OBSERVATIONS

The New Testament is a love story. A classic. The ultimate test of love was shown by Jesus Christ on a rugged, shameful cross of condemnation. Jesus put His own needs aside to be sure we had life offered to us. He lay down his life so we could live. By dying for all of us, Jesus showed the greatest demonstration of love. Christ's greatest command to us is to love one another as He has loved us.

ANECDOTE

"Adoption is the Loving Option" was the bumper sticker on my 1976 Buick Skylark over 20 years ago. Of all the bumper stickers out there, it was the one that I wanted others to read while waiting in traffic behind me. It made sense to me back then and it is the exact option one of my heroes recently chose.

Kate was thrown a double whammy. Years earlier she had been told she wouldn't be able to have children. At thirty-eight, she was definitely pregnant for the first time, not married yet and had learned this tiny surprise would be born with Down syndrome.

Kate wasn't sure she could handle being a mom of a healthy baby, but to complicate matters further, she had been told by professionals that 90 percent of these pregnancies were terminated. She decided to schedule an appointment for an abortion, thinking that was her only option but not a choice she was proud of.

Kate's partner, Greg, tried to support her decision and they headed to the appointment that would destroy their baby's young life. Suddenly, stopping the car, Greg confessed he couldn't do it...wouldn't do it. Kate was relieved. She was sick to her stomach from morning sickness or maybe it was fear. With Greg's love and support, she knew that she would not abort the growing baby inside her. Together, they knew there would be obstacles to overcome and they sought counseling from a parent group in their hometown.

"Unbelievable. Really?" Kate stated with relief when she learned there was a waiting list of families ready to adopt babies with Down syndrome. Knowing immediately that was a choice everyone could live with, quite literally, Kate and Greg began their search for a family to love their baby girl.

Taking the "high road," Kate lay down her life for this baby. She put her own needs aside in order to let her baby have life. There is no greater love than this. The day after Kate delivered our baby, I walked in to her hospital room to see this woman who had just gone through the trauma of childbirth holding my newborn daughter. My baby girl was being cradled in the arms of the woman who unselfishly gave her life in spite of personal agony. I knew that Kate loved this baby, too. In those moments, I knew that Kate and I were joined at the heart and baby Hope would be forever loved by two mommies - one born of the flesh and the other born of the heart.

INTAKE NOTES

Daily Dose 31 is the beginning of our story about our second daughter, Hope, who also has Down syndrome. As you just read, my daughter's birthmother was given hope when she learned there were families waiting to adopt children with special needs.

DIAGNOSTIC QUESTIONS

1. Have you ever thought about adopting?

2. What has been the outcome?

PRESCRIPTION FOR FOLLOW-UP

Maybe you or someone you know might be willing to join those of us who are learning the joys of adoption.

For further information on special needs adoption, here are a couple of websites for you to check out:
> www.chask.org (Christian Homes and Special Kids)
> www.dsagc/adoption.asp (Down Syndrome Association of Greater Cincinnati)

(2nd) PRESCRIPTION FOR FOLLOW-UP

I would love to hear from you personally!

1. Please let me know how **"Special Strength for Special Parents"** (that would be you) has impacted your life. My email is Nina@ninafuller.org

2. As we wrap up our 31 days of spiritual therapy together, where do you feel you have made progress:

   Emotionally:

   Spiritually:

3. Please be sure to include in your email which of the 31 Doses of Spiritual Therapy is/are your favorite(s) and which Parent Testimonial touched your heart.

4. I would also love to hear about YOUR loved one with special needs and how they have helped shape your life and brought you closer to God. Please send me your story. It just might become part of the next round of spiritual therapy!

What Makes Special Special

DawnDe Irwin

The impact of having a child with special needs in our family has been both a trial and a triumph. In the past, we had each known one or two people with disabilities. We weren't expecting the blessings and joy that were in store for us.

We knew before she was born that she had Down syndrome. I thought it was a blessing to know ahead of time as I was able to get most of the "'grieving" over the loss of having a "normal" child' done before she was born. Then I was able to make the transition to receive "the unending bundle of blessings" God had given our family. I remember the first time I saw her...she was so small (four pounds four ounces, six weeks early), so fragile, but at the same time she was a fighter, a survivor.

The roller coaster of emotions was rough. I remember thinking "SPECIAL," yeah, what is the meaning of the label "SPECIAL?" I was screaming inside, so angry. Who came up with this idea anyway? Why does the word SPECIAL apply to someone who has so many problems?

As time went on, therapy was started; she grew slowly, and I began to understand the meaning of being "special." Some might think that having a child with a disability would be a burden, but in truth I believe it is one of the most awesome blessings that could have been given to our family. Yes, we had some adjustments to make in our daily routines. And it does take a considerable amount of time and energy to attend all the appointments and services that are for her benefit. Sometimes it almost seems unfair to the kids without disabilities because there are so many opportunities to participate in activities.

This little girl is small in her physical stature, but she has a giant "heart full of love." There is a quality in her that is indeed a "special" gift. When strangers meet her they are immediately attracted to her. It's as if the Lord is touching them through her. She is so transparent. She is truly letting her "light shine" for the Lord.

I watch her and wonder what is going on in her mind. She is teaching me to be quicker to forgive. She gets over things so quickly and moves on to the next exciting thing happening. She is showing me how to get pleasure from the simple things in life. I no

175

longer wish to be in a hurry, "rushing" the day away. I am learning to enjoy living in the moment. The fact that her development is delayed and slow allows each step to be more fully experienced and appreciated.

She is a bundle of pure love and joy. She is so easy to be with, so warm and caring. She loves to dance and wrestle. She has an easy laugh. She is pure entertainment. We don't need to have the TV turned on or go anywhere!

I can't seem to find the words to express the love I feel when she puts her little arms around my neck and hugs me or when she kisses me, or when she puts her hands on her hips and shakes her "bootie."

What is it that makes her so special? Our family believes it is all the above qualities that make her "special." We now understand the meaning of "special" so well and get to embrace "special" with open arms.

EPILOGUE

The "special needs" world is one that I never would have entered on my own. It took an intentional act of God (a divine conception) to transport me to this different world in order for me to grow emotionally and spiritually. It has been a life-changing, chaotic, yet fulfilling, journey for me, Andy, and our family.

Shortly after Tess was born, a friend nicknamed her "Tess-timony." That is exactly what Joannah Tess Fuller has become in many ways. She is a testimony of God's faithfulness to those who trust Him. She is a testimony to our friends and family who have seen God at work in our lives. She is a testimony to you, new friends, who have followed my journey through the pages of **Special Strength for Special Parents.**

Because of Tess, our hearts were expanded to include another child with Down syndrome into our family through adoption. If not for Tess, we would not have precious Hope, our youngest daughter who is also wrapped up in a Down syndrome package. We have been gifted not once, but twice with these **special** gifts from the Lord.

Thank you for allowing me to enter your life and share my heart with you through **Special Strength for Special Parents.**

I pray that you and your **special** family are greatly blessed, my new and **special** friend!

~ Nina~

Appendix A
FEELINGS WORD LIST

Abandoned
Adamant
Adequate
Affectionate
Agony
Almighty
Amazed
Ambivalent
Angry
Annoyed
Anxious

Apathetic

Astounded

Awed

Bad
Beautiful
Betrayed
Bitter
Blissful
Bold
Bored
Brave
Burdened
Burned

Captivated
Cautious
Challenged
Charmed
Cheated
Cheerful
Childish
Clever
Competitive
Condemned
Confused

Conspicuous

Contented

Contrite

Cruel

Crushed

Culpable

Deceitful
Defeated
Deflated
Defused
Delighted
Desirous
Despair
Destructive
Determined
Different
Diffident

Diminished

Discontented

Distracted

Distraught

Disturbed

Divided

Dominated

Dubious

Eager
Ecstatic
Electrified
Empty
Enchanted
Energetic
Enjoy
Envious
Evil
Exasperated

Excited

Exhausted

Failure
Fascinated
Fawning
Fearful
Flustered
Foolish
Frantic
Free
Frightened
Frustrated

Full

Fury

Gay
Glad
Good
Gratified
Greedy
Grief
Groovy
Guilty
Gullible

Happy
Hate
Heavenly
Helpful
High
Homesick
Honored
Horrible
Hurt
Hysterical

Ignored
Immortal
Imposed upon
Impressed
Indignant
Infatuated
Inferior
Infuriated
Inspired

Intimidated

Isolated

Jealousy
Joyous
Jumpy

Keen
Kinky
Kind

Laconic
Lazy
Lecherous
Left out
Licentious
Lonely
Longing
Loving
Low

Mad
Maudlin
Mean
Melancholy
Miffed
Miserable
Misunderstood
Mystical

Naughty	Obnoxious	Pain	Precarious
Nervous	Obsessed	Panicked	Pressured
Nice	Odd	Parsimonious	Pretty
Nitpicky	Opposed	Peaceful	Prim
Nutty	Outraged	Persecuted	Proud
	Overwhelmed	Petrified	
		Pity	
		Pleasant	Quarrelsome
		Pleased	Queer

Rage	Sad	Talkative	Vehement
Rapture	Sated	Tempted	Vengeful
Redundant	Satisfied	Tenacious	Violent
Refreshed	Scared	Tense	Vital
Rejected	Screwed up	Tentative	Vitality
Relaxed	Servile	Terrible	Vivacious
Relieved	Sexy	Terrified	Vulnerable
Remorse	Shaky	Threatened	
Restless	Shocked	Thwarted	
Reverent	Silly	Tired	Weepy
Rewarded	Skeptical	Trapped	Wicked
Righteous	Sneaky	Troubled	Wonderful
Robbed	Solemn		Worry
	Sorrowful		
	Spiteful	Ugly	Zany
	Startled	Uneasy	
	Stingy	Unloved	
	Stuffed	Unsettled	
	Stunned	Upset	
	Stupefied		
	Stupid		
	Suffering		
	Sure		
	Sympathetic		

RESOURCES

www.childrenofdestiny.org

www.bandofangels.com

www.hydrocephalus.com

www.joubertsyndrome.org

www.torticollis.org

www.nami.org/www.world-schizophrenia.org

www.health.groups.yaho.com/grouop/chromosome8/

www.dev.delay.org

www.epilepsyfoundation.org

www.ndss.org

www.sinetwork.org – autism

www.sbaa.org

www.einstein-syndrome.com

www.dsagc.com – Adoption Awareness Program for Children with
Down syndrome:
or call Robin Steele – 513.761.5400

www.chask.org - Christian Homes And Special Kids - Adoption of
children with
Special Needs

www.metlife.com/metdesk

www.arc.com

www.lisatuttle.com

www.pujolsfamilyfoundation.org

AUTHOR INFORMATION

Nina Fuller is the founder of Living Proof Testimonies and S.M.I.L.E. on Down Syndrome. She is a nationally popular speaker and author and shares full time ministry responsibilities with her husband, Andy. Add her personal life experiences for good measure and you get a woman of God who knows her purpose in life and exactly where her strength comes from and it's not from herself.

Nina is a gifted Bible teacher, spiritual counselor, and mentor to teens and adults.

The Fullers have five children, two of whom have Down syndrome.

Nina's website is:
www.NinaFuller.org

For speaking engagements, Nina can be reached by contacting Ambassador Speakers Bureau, Franklin, TN ~ 615/370-4700 or info@AmbassadorAgency.com